SIR JAMES GUNN

SPONSORED BY

BAILLIE GIFFORD & CO

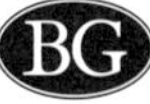

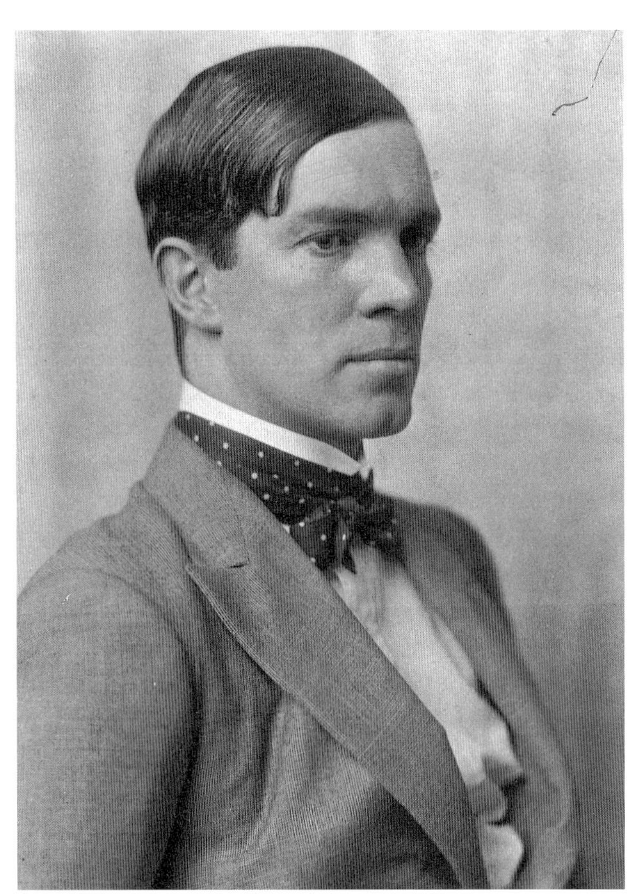

SIR JAMES

GUNN

1893 – 1964

SCOTTISH

NATIONAL PORTRAIT

GALLERY

1994

Published 1994 by the
Trustees of the National Galleries of Scotland
for the exhibition held at the Scottish National Portrait Gallery,
Edinburgh, 3 December 1994 to 26 February 1995,
The Fine Art Society, London, 13 March to 21 April 1995,
and at the Harris Museum and Art Gallery, Preston,
15 May to 1 July 1995.

© *The authors and the Trustees of the National Galleries of Scotland 1994*

ISBN 0 903598 52 3

Designed & typeset in Monotype Fournier by Dalrymple
Printed and bound by BAS Printers Ltd
Over Wallop, Hampshire

Frontispiece: James Gunn
Photographed by T. & R. Annan & Sons, Glasgow, c.1923
Front Cover: Pauline in the Yellow Dress, 1944, cat. 58
Back Cover: Self-portrait, 1941, cat. 57

Foreword 7

Gunn on Gunn 9
 Sir James Gunn

Sir James Gunn 1893–1964 13
 Richard Ingleby

Sir James Gunn and the Royal Academy 23
 Mary Anne Stevens

A Memoir 29
 Chloë Gunn

Chronology 35
 Petronella Gunn

Colour Plates 41

Catalogue of Exhibits 65

Bibliography 79

FOREWORD

T H E portraits of James Gunn were exhibited regularly, and usually to considerable acclaim, at the Royal Academy in London and the Royal Scottish Academy in Edinburgh during a career that stretched from 1929 until his death in 1964. Gunn had not set out to be a portrait painter, but when he changed direction in the former year the way was set for the rest of his life. It was a path that brought him immense success, including many public honours, although, curiously, his full membership of the Royal Academy did not come until 1961. The realistic nature of his portraiture gained wide acceptance in what might be termed establishment circles and it is doubtful if much attention was paid in the many board rooms where it was hung to any of its underlying formal qualities. And in later years, when virtually any form of figurative art became suspect, and when the tenets of modernism seemed unassailable, his reputation suffered greatly, a situation that has tended to persist since his death thirty years ago.

However, attitudes and horizons change ineluctably and we believe the time is ripe to look afresh at the virtues that have gone unregarded in Gunn's work. The exhibition begins with a number of his early works, made in the years before the decisive switch to commissioned portraiture. These show a fluent, creative painter with gifts that might seem at variance with his later practice when the demands of the board room had to be answered. It is our belief, however, that the exhibition will demonstrate that his work was more of a complete whole than was once thought, especially now that we can take a more relaxed view of the kind of factual realism that his portraiture represented.

The exhibition has been curated by James Holloway, Assistant Keeper of the Scottish National Portrait Gallery. He, in turn, has worked closely with Richard Ingleby of The Fine Art Society, an expert on twentieth-century British art. They would particularly like to acknowledge the cordial and fruitful co-operation of members of the artist's family and, in particular, the continuous help they have received from Chloë and Paul Gunn.

It is a particular pleasure that the exhibition has been sponsored by the Edinburgh-based company Baillie Gifford, the largest independently owned investment firm in

Scotland. Their generosity has enabled us to borrow from far afield and to produce a lavishly illustrated catalogue which will remain as a colourful souvenir of the exhibition and a memorial of the artist's work.

Many other people have contributed substantially to this exhibition and we would like to thank the following: the Atelier de Restauration des Photographies de la ville de Paris (for restoring the photograph of Gunn by Dorothy Wilding, fig. 6); Petronella Gunn; Robin Hutchison; Christopher MacLehose; Andrew McIntosh Patrick; David Paul Ltd; MaryAnne Stevens; Donald Swan; Carol Willoughby; Liz Young.

After the exhibition closes in Edinburgh it will be shown at The Fine Art Society in London, a firm which actively promoted Gunn's work during his lifetime and has continued to do so ever since. A selection from the exhibition will subsequently be presented at the Harris Museum and Art Gallery in Preston. This final showing has been made possible by an award under the Business Sponsorship Incentive Scheme, the Government Scheme administered by the Association for Business Sponsorship of the Arts.

Finally, we would like to acknowledge the generosity of all the lenders to this exhibition who have parted with their paintings for many months. Their readiness to share them has enabled us to bring the work of James Gunn once more to a wide audience.

TIMOTHY CLIFFORD
Director, National Galleries of Scotland

DUNCAN THOMSON
Keeper, Scottish National Portrait Gallery

GUNN ON GUNN

Taken from the text of a speech made by Gunn at the Glasgow Art Club, 18 November 1955

I HAVE always insisted that no after dinner speech should last for more than five minutes, preferably three. Imagine my consternation when Percy Bliss suggested at least half an hour for the duration of this effort. It is difficult to be a bore in three minutes, but practically impossible not to be in half an hour.

If I am to talk for so long, the only subject that will hold out, about which I know enough, is myself. I wonder, can you take it?

Someone asked me recently, what was my first portrait? I can't recall a time when I didn't draw, but my first portrait, so far as I can fix it, was done when I was six. It was of my father, full length, sitting cross-legged, reading his newspaper, and was drawn on slate, one of those convenient, but unhygienic articles no longer in use. When I showed it to him he said: 'Why didn't you draw that in your book, if you had I would have given you 6d.' That was something I never forgot, but I have no recollection of any financial profit accruing.

My first mentor was my father's old friend and mine, Brownlie Docharty. On Saturday mornings I went to Blythswood Square where I shaded cubes and spheres and painted water colours of daffodils. Later my Saturdays were spent at the School of Art, in the time of that picturesque Whistleresque predecessor of Bliss, Francis H. Newbery, a considerable personality and no mean painter. Soon after this I took to portrait painting and learnt a lot from copying the Raeburns at Kelvingrove.

It was in 1908 that my father took me to London with a selection of my portraits to an appointment with the President of the Royal Academy, Sir Edward Poynter. He had written inviting us to call, but remarking that in these days he would advise no young man to pursue a career in art if he did not possess private means … I remember the visit to that studio in Addison Road; there was a butler to show us in. On an easel was a portrait of Edward VII that I have since seen hanging on some unflattering wall in the depths of Burlington House for which it was painted. The President looked at my portraits, then taking my father by the arm, led him to a distance, but not as he thought out of hearing of my young ears, and I heard him say 'You must give this boy a chance'. From this interview we went to Little Campden House on Campden Hill, with an introduction to the Keeper of the Royal Academy, Sir Arthur Cope, who received us, and after some kindly criticism advised my father to send me to the Royal Academy Schools.

In the end I went to Edinburgh. One of the best things to come out of that experience was an enduring friendship with a fellow student, Bill Hutchison. We foregathered again in Paris and I imagine he too remembers those walks in the small hours between my little studio in the Rue Perrel and his more sophisticated quarters in the neighbourhood of the Luxembourg. When the long way was not long enough we retraced it again and again and talked and talked and all the world was ours.

… In Paris I studied at the Académie Julian under Jean-Paul Laurens. The academic standard was high, if you won a *concour* there you were quite a draughtsman. I returned from Paris with a collection of sketches made in the streets and by the river. Many of these passed through the house of Annan. There they were seen and some were purchased by a dealer from Bond Street, W. B. Paterson, brother of the distinguished Scottish Academician, James. He gave me a contract, paid me a retaining fee and I undertook to provide him with not less than thirty pictures a year, he taking 50% of the sales which suited me very well. At his instigation I went to Spain at the beginning of 1914. There I travelled, seeing and painting, till the echoes from Sarajevo warned that the good days were soon to end.

… I had an undistinguished career in the army, serving mainly with the 10th Scottish Rifles, 15th Division, and by the time I got back into circulation, most of the hot money that had made for a boom in the arts was already dissipated. I went south and entered on my years of struggle, exploited my credit to the limit, entertained my quota of bailiffs, all the usual features of a career that calls for a lot of faith.

… In 1932 I sent a group portrait to the Royal Academy, a conversation piece of Belloc, Chesterton and Maurice Baring. One morning I received a 'phone call at my studio from someone who said: 'You don't know me, my name is Cope, and I have just come from the Royal Academy – it is members' varnishing day. I left many of them gathered around your picture and I felt I would like to tell you, I think you have painted a masterpiece'. Overwhelmed, I assured him we had met and reminded him of the occasion. He said: 'You must come and see me, I have often wondered what happened to that boy.'

Such generosity is rare in our trade, but I met it in the men of that generation, James Guthrie, E. A. Walton and John Lavery, great men all.

One of my first patrons, a dear friend and great connoisseur of the arts, was Arthur

Kay. He bought a number of sketches from my
Paris days and in the early 30s when I revisited
Edinburgh to paint the late Professor Robertson,
I seized the chance to paint Kay and left the portrait with him. At Aitken Dott's where he took it
for framing it was seen by another connoisseur,
Kenneth Sanderson. He wrote congratulating
Kay on the portrait and enquiring about the
painter. Then when the great engineering house
of Balfour Beatty & Co wanted to celebrate its
coming of age with portraits of the founders,
George Balfour sought advice from Sanderson
who sent him to me. A great friendship grew out

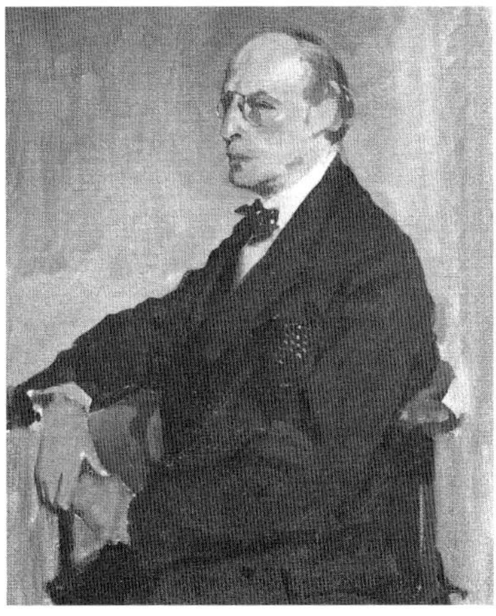

fig. 1

Arthur Kay

Scottish National

Portrait Gallery

of this and George Balfour bought amongst other works the Conversation Piece of
which I have spoken and which is now at the National Portrait Gallery. He bought too
my portrait of Delius, later acquired by the City of Bradford, at, I am glad to say, considerable profit to his heirs.

Some of you must have heard the BBC critics on portraiture at the RA. They make
me rage, but I sometimes listen. One of them remarked, 'I suppose the least important
thing about a portrait is that it should be like the subject, what does it matter in fifty
years'. This passed unchallenged. Of what else dare one say, the least important thing
is that it should fulfil its function? We have, of course, our compensations, we make
interesting contact with the great, the Royal, the noble, the successful and the
beautiful.

… I had thought to recount some of these tales, but I must be near my limit, I will
save them for that book I'll never write.

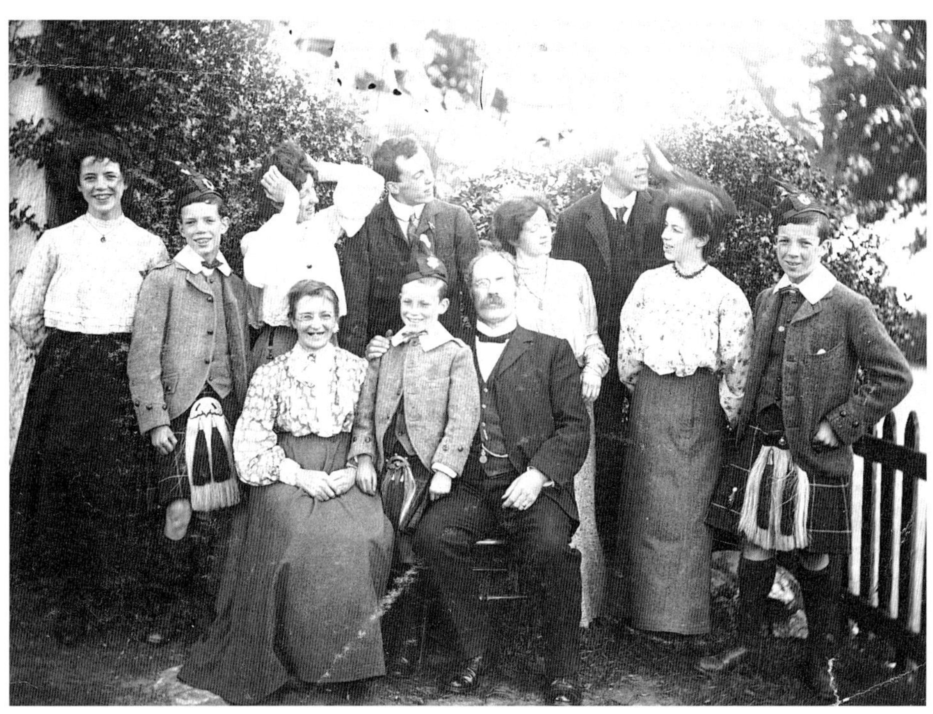

fig. 2 Richard and Thomasina Gunn and their family, about 1904. James Gunn is second from the left.

SIR JAMES GUNN
1893–1964

JAMES GUNN, who died at the age of 71 on 30 December 1964, chose not to write an autobiography despite, at the end of his life, the encouragement of several publishers eager for the chance to eavesdrop at his studio door. He was, in the middle years of the twentieth century, this country's leading portrait painter, privy to the company of one King, two Queens, four Prime Ministers, several Generals (including Montgomery, in his caravan in Belgium during the Second World War) as well as countless other statesmen, industrialists, artists, writers, academics and the occasional fisherman. With them all he insisted on conversation, on the principle that to look interesting the subject had to be interested: 'My paintings are conversation pieces in the proper sense.'[1] Gunn's memoirs of these sittings would have made interesting reading, a mini-history of our times as seen from the artist's studio, words to match the pictures which themselves record nearly half a century. As it is, the speech that Gunn made to the Glasgow Art Club in November 1955 was the closest he came to publishing an account of his life.

The Royal Academy has a part to play in the career of any portrait painter, and few more so than James Gunn. From his first encounter, at the age of 15, with the wealth and grandeur of its President to the invitation to be its Treasurer fifty-six years[2] later the Academy was a constant presence in his life.

After 1935[3] the annual exhibitions of the Royal Academy, the Royal Scottish Academy, the Royal Glasgow Institute of the Fine Arts and the Royal Society of Portrait Painters were Gunn's only opportunity to have his work judged objectively by the general public. Of these the Royal Academy in London reached by far the largest audience. Throughout his long career Gunn's art was repeatedly acknowledged by the public. His were the pictures that they went to the Academy to see[4] and which were judged by the Press as having '… the complexion which one has come to regard as Royal Academic'.[5]

Why it should have taken so long for them to elect him as one of their own is an important question, and one that is addressed by MaryAnne Stevens in her essay, 'Sir James Gunn and The Royal Academy'. It is enough here to note the importance that the Academy always had for Gunn, and that his continual exclusion throughout the 1930s and '40s was a source of sadness to him, and of bewilderment to the world at large.

Another significant year that Gunn might have mentioned in his autobiography was 1929. This was the year of his exhibition, predominantly of landscapes, at The Fine Art Society. He was, at the time, contemplating marriage to Pauline Miller, the woman who became his second wife in August of that year.[6] He wrote to her on 22 February: 'I haven't been near the show, it depresses me to keep on going and finding nothing sold. I can't understand the public. None of my really good things have gone yet. I know so well that if things are going they go from the start. There seems to be something about my work that doesn't appeal. I wonder what it is. The Italian woman (Emma Ciardi) who had a show of Venice pictures, poor stuff, sold ninety-five. So far I have sold three'. His tally didn't improve, but meanwhile the critic of the *Daily Telegraph* noted that '… the artist seems sometimes to be at his best when painting portraits. There is ease of handling and a certain pleasurable richness of expression in a portrait such as that of Mr H. Belloc. H. J. Gunn leaves us in no doubt that he has that first and indispensable quality of the true portrait painter and of translating that observation into terms of paint.'

On 15 March he wrote to Pauline, in better spirits, and described a new portrait that he had begun of the actor Charles Pond (cat. 43, plate 13): 'Bill Hutchison [his old friend from student days and an accomplished portrait painter] says it is the finest thing I've ever done and makes him feel like giving up his job.' It was a crucial moment, a watershed, and coincidentally it came exactly half way through his life, almost to the

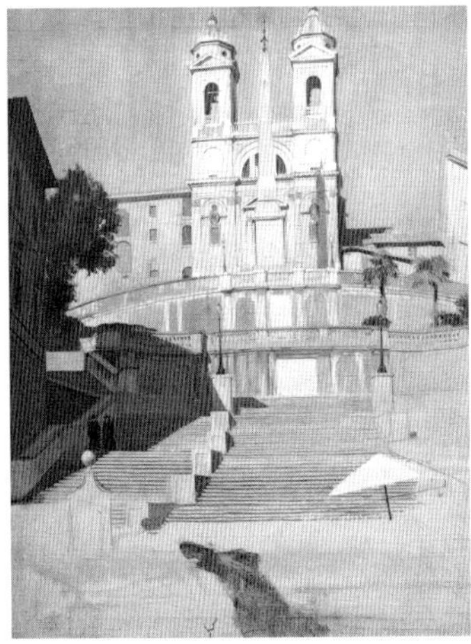

day. He made the decision to devote his career to portraiture, a decision on which his life turned. A view of the Trinità dei Monti, which had been unfinished when he returned to London from Rome for the start of The Fine Art Society's exhibition, remained in his studio, unfinished (fig. 3).

Up to this point Gunn's energies had been divided between portraiture and landscape but it was his landscapes that had been the basis of his first seriously commercial commission. In Paris in 1912 he had begun to paint small, tonally delicate panels: Whistlerian street scenes and views of public gardens peopled by tiny figures made by a few wispy strokes of the brush (cf. cat. 6, plate 1). Some of these were seen by the London dealer W. B. Paterson who in 1914 commissioned Gunn to travel through Spain to North Africa, intending to exhibit the pictures in London on Gunn's return.

Paterson was the brother of the 'Glasgow Boy' James Paterson and a forward-thinking dealer, responsible for the exhibition of French Impressionist pictures in Glasgow in November 1912,[7] an exhibition which Gunn presumably saw. Gunn already had some experience of France, but was encouraged to look further afield, specifically to Spain where he discovered Velázquez who remained an influence, second only to Raeburn, throughout his life.

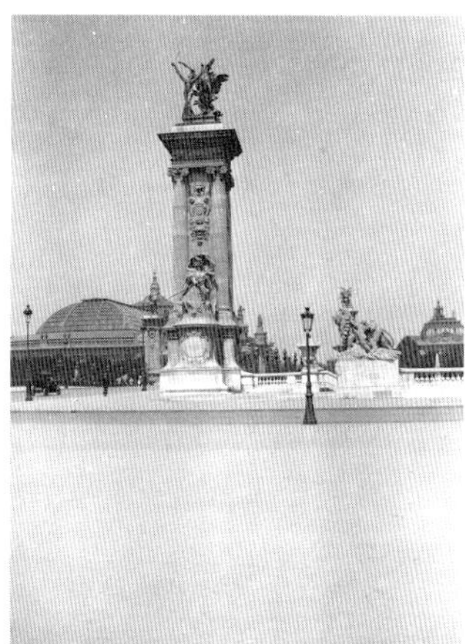

fig. 4
Pont d'Alexandre, Paris
Photograph taken by James Gunn in 1913

Paterson may also have been responsible for providing Gunn with a Kodak camera, or at least for suggesting that its judicious use could be an added tool in the bag of the *plein air* painter (figs. 4 and 5).[8] There is an element of the snapshot in the composition of many of these early landscapes, and the photographs that he took must have helped with his understanding of tonal distribution. Only very rarely did it get the better of him. His technical abilities took him far beyond any need to use the camera as a short cut and he seems to have given it up all together after his travels were curtailed by the advent of war in 1914.

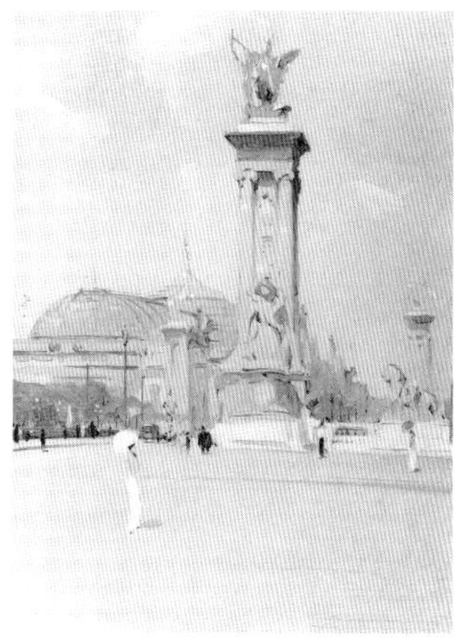

fig. 5
Pont d'Alexandre, Paris
Private Collection

Paterson re-opened his Bond Street gallery in June 1919 with an exhibition of fifty-two of Gunn's landscapes. This was followed in November by an exhibition of the pictures unsold in London at the galleries of T. & R. Annan & Sons in Glasgow. This pattern of showing first in London and then in Glasgow developed throughout the 1920s and led to continual confusion in the Press about Gunn's standing in the world of art. When he showed in London he was described as a young man well known at home in Scotland, but yet to make his mark in the south. When he showed in Glasgow he was the local boy riding on the back of his London success. His reputation took a boost on both sides of the border in 1924 when his portrait of James Pryde was exhibited at the Royal

Glasgow Institute and sold for £450 to the Scottish Modern Arts Association.

His pictures of Pryde (there were three in all), of Bill Hutchison (cat. 41), and Hutchison's of him[9] share a certain poise. They combine the look of the gentleman artist – hats, gloves, canes and coats – with that of the Scotsman on the make. This, of course, they were, in as much as they knew where they were going. It was a point which was made in the Press in response to the portraits of Belloc and Pond in the Royal Academy in 1929: 'I heard some idiot say that this is the coming Orpen, which he isn't, but the coming James Gunn'.[10]

By 1932 when a second portrait of James Pryde (cat. 46, plate 14) was hung at the annual exhibition of the Royal Society of Portrait Painters and *Conversation Piece* (cat. 47, plate 15) appeared at the Royal Academy, the Scottish Press were proud to be claiming a triumph for 'the famous Scottish artist'.[11] The *Daily Telegraph* noted that ' ... if *Conversation Piece* had not already been sold for £1,500 to a private purchaser, the Chantrey Trustees would certainly have acquired it.'[12] The private purchaser was George Balfour, whom Gunn had painted the previous year and who subsequently became his greatest patron.

Conversation Piece was well titled. Belloc, Baring, Chesterton and Gunn became good friends and can seldom have been short of words in each other's company. The idea for the painting had been conceived between them at Belloc's sixtieth-birthday party in 1930, but its realisation had taken nearly two years. Even then it was rare for Gunn to get them all in the studio at once, and they left doodled messages for each other from one sitting to the next. Together they wrote a lament for the trees which were then being cut down in Cheyne Row – *The Ballade of Devastation*, composed by Baring and Chesterton 'with interpretations by Hilaire Belloc'. It was scribbled on the back of one of Chesterton's drawings, dated 15 February, and appeared in *The Times* the next day.[13]

> *They're breaking down the bridge at Waterloo;*
> *They've daubed the house of Henry James at Rye;*
> *They've caught a man and put him in the Zoo;*
> *They've let the Japanese into Shanghai;*
> *They may destroy St Peter's (on the sly);*
> *They all agree that dogma has to go;*
> *From pole to pole the shattered temples lie;*
> *They're cutting down the trees in Cheyne Row.*

The painting process wasn't always so easy, or so enjoyable. At the end of 1932 Gunn travelled to Grez-sur-Loing to paint the aged and blind composer Delius (cat. 53, plate 16). He had wanted to paint his portrait since first seeing him at the Queen's Hall in 1929, but when the occasion arose he found that there was little time for conversation between artist and sitter. Delius was very infirm and would only sit for two hours each afternoon, a régime which hindered Gunn's customary and very deliberate working method.

'When I start a new portrait I spend the first sitting making a preliminary sketch. This doesn't commit me, it gives me the chance to study my subject, and it gives him time to study me, and to find out that being painted isn't such an ordeal, he becomes relaxed. I use a canvas 18" by 14", this approximates to the dimensions of most portrait sizes. I fix proportion accordingly and make a quick first impression. If the result seems right I scale it up, if not I may have seen in the course of the sitting what I do want. The point is that I like to start with a definite idea of design and placing, and stick to it. Of course, as you work, you will often see something, a turn of the head, and think how much better that is. You change, you start again, only to find the new conception is not better, only different. That is a great snare.'[14]

In April 1929 he had written to Pauline of his desire for a normal working life, painting portraits daily 'from ten till six like the working man'. By 1933 the lifestyle Gunn had wished for was in place. He arrived promptly at the studio every morning in a black jacket, tie and pin-striped trousers and, having swopped his jacket for a clean painting coat and check-ed his appointments with his secretary, began work on the first canvas of the day (fig. 6). Despite some of his Savage Club friendships the concept of artist as Bohemian was not for him. Gunn was a professional and as such was fiercely proud of his profession. It was, he said, 'a rather special branch of art, it calls for a peculiar and somewhat rare

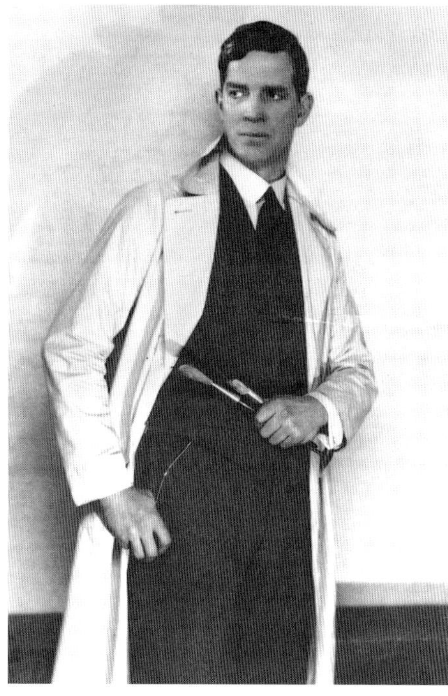

fig. 6
James Gunn
Photograph by
Dorothy Wilding

talent in addition to a degree of skill and draughtsmanship obviously not required in other directions'.[15] But he was also keenly aware of falling standards.

'The camera has had a great effect on portrait painting, it has imposed a higher standard of likeness, but it has opened the way to many who, without its aid, would not be in the game, some painters of repute, no names. They argue that what counts is the result, not the means, that it is the invention of the age, that Holbein would have used it, that it saves time in this hectic age, and so on. But, is the man who works the pianola, with whatever skill, to be counted among the virtuosi? The pianola finds the notes as the camera finds the drawing, and in my submission they are in the same category, yet unless seen on the job it isn't easy to detect the fraud.'[16]

Donald Swan, who worked for Gunn in the early 1950s making portrait copies, describes him as the most modest of men: 'I found his complete lack of vanity constant and very becoming in him. It was a great virtue'.[17] He recalled watching his employer at work. It was a remarkable technique, moving across a yard or more of canvas in the space of an afternoon, one brush stroke going down next to the last, side by side – no under-painting, no glazing, no scumbling, thinning or rubbing. Small sables were used only for the minutest details – for ordinary painting it was hog filberts. It was what Gunn called 'the principle of thin painting'. When Swan asked him how he did it, Gunn replied, 'I just bash it on'. Swan continues: 'This was hard to believe, for his pictures looked as if they had been French polished. They certainly didn't look "bashed on". But they were, I saw him do it … for each brush stroke he took a small amount of pure paint on the palette and brushed it directly on to the canvas, hardly fusing with the previous one as they were so close in value and colour. Each brush stroke was quite separate and never to be touched again. That was the secret of his thin paint – never needing to be painted over. As he said, absolutely direct painting – bashing it on.'[18]

It was this combination of assured touch and brilliant observation that gave rise to portraits like that of Harold Macmillan (cat. 70, plate 23). Even at the end of his career Gunn had lost none of his technique and in a two-hour sitting he produced what was effectively a finished portrait. 'It seemed so complete that I decided to leave it, and copy the arrangement on to a new canvas for the second sitting.'[19]

It may also have given rise to a degree of professional jealousy among his contemporaries. Gunn was simply too good at what he did. His confidence behind the easel was too much for one 'minor celebrity', 'who had been done before'. After watching Gunn sketch away busily for some time he became impatient. 'Young man', he said severely, 'I'll have you know I have been painted already by two Royal Academicians and they both brought cameras. Can you not afford one?'[20]

This was a story that Gunn liked to tell, but it was dangerously close to the bone. Donald Swan recalls Gunn's anger in 1944 on hearing Gerald Kelly's dismissal of *Pauline in the Yellow Dress* (cat. 58, plate 18) as 'cheap and photographic'. It was the ultimate insult. 'The bastard', he said, 'he'd be lost without his Leica'. Kelly was one of those members of the artistic establishment who had their place in the Royal Academy, but also had cause to envy Gunn's popularity with the public. On the face of it Kelly should have been Gunn's natural ally within the Academy, yet it seems that quite the opposite was true, and his place on the selection committee of 1942 may well have had something to do with its rejection that year of all of Gunn's submissions. It is possible, as MaryAnne Stevens notes,[21] that two years of total rejection (1935 and 1942) may have counted against Gunn and delayed his election to the Academy, but it also seems likely that the rejection of his work and delay in gaining membership were symptoms of the same thing, namely the jealousy of his contemporaries. Year after year it was Gunn's portraits, specifically those of Pauline, that appeared in the pages of *Tatler*, *Bystander* and the *Sketch* and which found most favour with the public at the summer exhibition. He was simply too successful to join the club.

Pauline in the Yellow Dress, unharmed by Kelly's snub, was bought for £1000 by the Harris Art Gallery, Preston, within an hour of the Royal Academy opening (and soon after, according to the *Sunday Chronicle*, someone else was offering twice the price). It was, in the words of the *Daily Mail*, 'the Mona Lisa of 1944' and the public voted it 'Picture of the Year'. The *Daily Mail*'s correspondent continued: '… experts told me that he has been up for election four times … but has just been unlucky'.

It was starting to look like more than bad luck. In fact Sydney Paviere, Preston Corporation's Art Director, identified the problem unwittingly in his praise of the picture they had bought. 'I feel it was the most technically perfect picture of the Academy, with painter-like qualities recalling the best works of the pre-war years'. This was the problem. Gunn's work seemed to epitomise everything about the years before the Second World War, years that were now being left behind. He was very definitely of the old school without being part of it, and meanwhile there was another faction eager to modernise the Academy and keep the likes of Gunn out.

Official honours may have been slow to come his way, but Gunn had no shortage of distinguished commissions throughout the 1940s and 1950s. It was to his studio that the King walked, in full uniform, because the official car was too wide for the

Kensington mews,[22] and it was he who received a telephone call from the War Office one August evening in 1944, and who ten days later was painting General Montgomery in the field. Among the pictures that he brought back from this impromptu trip to France and Belgium was a small canvas depicting the Commander-in-Chief with his personal staff and pet rabbit in their mess-tent (fig. 7). When this picture was shown at the Academy in 1945 the critic Adrian Bury described it as 'not just a rapid and skilful piece of painting, but a historic document of importance'.[23] Increasingly that is what Gunn's pictures became, historic documents of both private (cat. 71) and public (cat. 67) significance.

Until his eventual election as an associate member of the Royal Academy in 1953, the possibility of rejection from the summer exhibition remained a recurring anxiety, though gradually it also became something Gunn could joke about. In 1950 he submit-

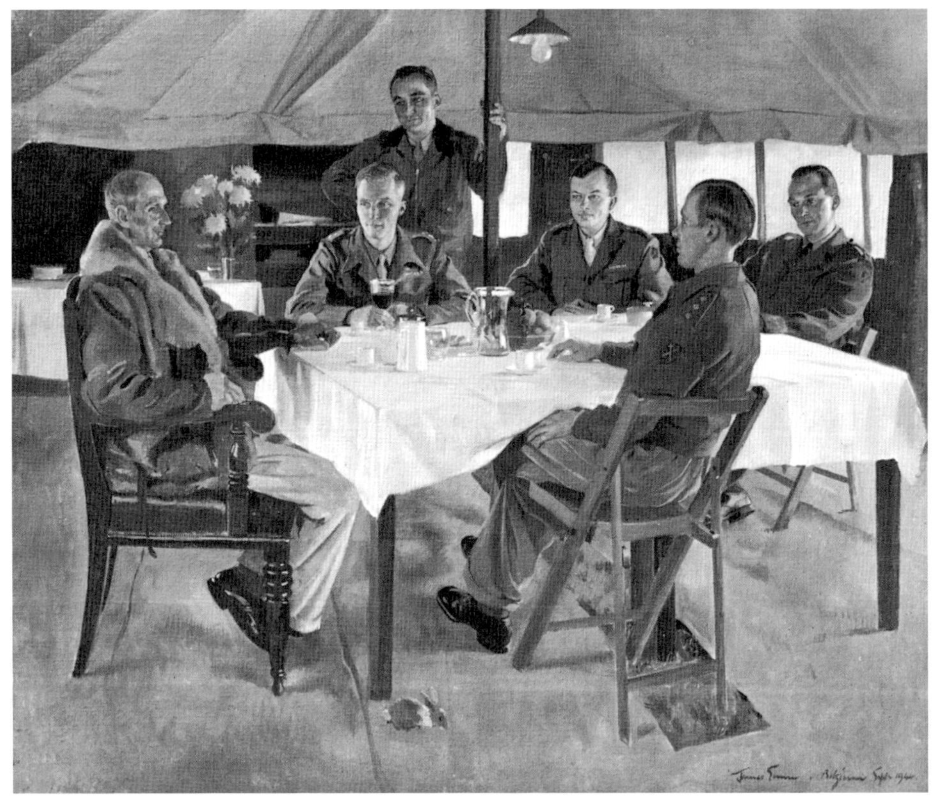

fig. 7
Field-Marshal Montgomery with members of his personal staff in the mess-tent, Belgium, September 1944
Her Majesty, Queen Elizabeth, The Queen Mother

ted an informal portrait of the Royal Family, *Conversation Piece at Royal Lodge Windsor* (cat. 67, plate 22) and a portrait of the Lord Mayor of London, warning its subject not to be surprised if it wasn't accepted: ' ... as for the other one, even Kelly won't be able to throw that out, even if it's late – when it comes from Windsor'.[24]

Official honours trickled in towards the end of Gunn's life, including the Presidency of the Royal Society of Portrait Painters, an honorary degree from the University of Glasgow and honorary citizenship of the State of Texas. He was finally made a full member of the Academy in 1961 and awarded a knighthood for his services to the arts in 1963.

James Gunn died during the night of Wednesday 30 December 1964 in the King Edward VII Hospital for Officers in London, after a three-week illness. Obituary notices appeared as far afield as the *New York Times* and the *Plymouth Evening News*. In the *Daily Telegraph* Humphrey Brooke, the Secretary of the Royal Academy, was reported as saying that ' ... these pictures will now be seen to place Gunn above Orpen and on the level of Sargent'. Sir Charles Wheeler, the President of the Academy, said simply: 'He painted history'.

'The art of portraiture', Hilaire Belloc wrote in his introduction to Gunn's 1933 exhibition at Barbizon House, ' ... demands two things: a picture and a representation of the human soul.' Gunn's own estimation of his art was more humble. The soul was not his territory. Brilliance of execution and observation were the best that an honest portrait painter could aspire to: 'An Artist does not need to be a judge of

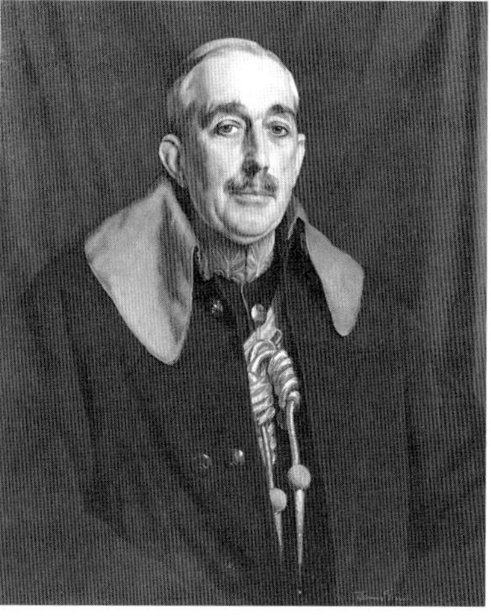

fig. 8
The Earl of Clanwilliam
The Carlton Club

character if he paints what he sees and paints it sincerely. Orpen, the greatest of us all, said that a real portraitist does not form an idea of his subject's character and then paint the face to match it, and he was right. On this point I will tell you a little story. I was painting a certain titled man of long descent (fig. 8) and half way through the sittings I detected on the canvas a resemblance to the likeness of Cardinal Richelieu, the great French statesman of Louis XIII's era. I spoke to the sitter and he saw the resemblance too. It turned out that in the seventeenth century a far off ancestress of the man I was painting had come very much into Richelieu's life.'[25]

Back in 1929, the year that changed Gunn's life, Belloc had made a more personal response to seeing a portrait of himself on show in the Royal Academy: 'Dear Gunn, Joy. Fun. Excellent. Admirable. It shows their taste. And to me it is particularly gratifying. I want the attention. Time presses. I'm 59. I shall put on a mask and go and listen to the comments of the public. … It's a great thing to have one's picture painted by a man of genius like you because posterity then knows all about it. They say "nothing is known of the man save his magnificent portrait by Gunn" or they say "Portrait of an unknown person by Gunn". Sometimes they go as far as to say "Portrait of a Gentleman". They can only do that by the clothes. Yours H. B.'

Gunn's own response to posterity was, characteristically, more humble. At the time of his election to the Royal Academy in 1961 the *Daily Mail* correspondent asked him what he thought his work would add up to in the end: ' … Gunn pondered. Then he said: "Men like Augustus John broadened people's vision. I don't think I have done that. I just hope that something of what I have done will survive".'[26]

It has survived. Gunn's greatest contribution, like all good portrait painters, has been to history. He believed that 'portraiture at its highest should achieve all that painting is capable of, in addition to its portrait interest'. In his best work, in his portraits of Hilaire Belloc or James Pryde, or of his wife Pauline, Gunn achieved that goal.

1. Donald Swan, Memories of James Gunn. Manuscript letter to the author (p.6).

2. Gunn died before taking up the position.

3. Except for a final one man show of *First Impressions* at Thomas Agnew & Sons in 1946.

4. His works were frequently contenders for the 'Picture of the Year'. In 1944 *Pauline in the Yellow Dress* won the title.

5. *Apollo*, June 1933.

6. Gunn's marriage to Gwendoline Hillman had been dissolved in 1927.

7. Held at the Grand Hotel, November 1912.

8. His brother James was a case in point.

9. In the collection of the Royal Scottish Academy.

10. *Sporting Times*, 11 May 1929.

11. *Glasgow Referee*, 1 May 1932.

12. *Daily Telegraph*, 30 April 1932.

13. *The Times*, 16 February 1932.

14. Sybil Vincent, 'In the studio of James Gunn', *The Studio*, December 1936.

15. Notes for a speech.

16. Ibid.

17. Swan, p.10.

18. Swan, p.10. The description of watching Gunn paint relates to his painting a background. Swan was never in the studio at the same time as a sitter.

19. Cf. cat. 70.

20. Sybil Vincent, loc. cit.

21. MaryAnne Stevens, 'Sir James Gunn and The Royal Academy'.

22. *7 Tagge*, published in Germany, 1950. Manuscript translation in the Gunn collection.

23. *Daily Dispatch*, 5 May 1945.

24. Swan, p.14.

25. Vaughan Dryden, 'Celebrities in the Studio' (article in untraced journal).

26. *Daily Mail*, 23 February 1961.

M A R Y A N N E   S T E V E N S

SIR JAMES GUNN AND THE ROYAL ACADEMY

$\mathbf{A}$T THE Royal Academy's summer exhibition of 1932, James Gunn showed *Conversation Piece* (cat. 47, plate 15).[1] In a meticulous, sharply-handled technique Gunn placed around a highly polished table the figures of three leading men of letters, Hilaire Belloc, Maurice Baring and G. K. Chesterton. Relatively casually posed, against a background of seeming informality which suggests execution in the artist's studio (part of an empty picture frame stands propped on the right-hand side as if awaiting the picture's completion), the painting was the only one to be shown by Gunn that year. It was received with great acclaim, becoming, as was noted in a later article on the artist, 'the sensation of the Academy Exhibition of 1932'.[2] Indeed, according to Gunn's own account given in 1955, he had received a telephone call from Sir Arthur Cope, on the morning of the members' varnishing day, in which the distinguished senior Academician had reported that he had 'left many of them [the members] gathered around your picture and I felt I would like to tell you, I think you have painted a masterpiece.'[3]

Such a laudatory reception for *Conversation Piece* requires further investigation, both through placing the painting within the perspective of Gunn's own work and within a broader context of the artist's immediate predecessors and contemporaries. It also raises the more problematic issue of Gunn's relationship with the Royal Academy of Arts, since, despite this acclaim, he remained excluded from membership of that institution for a further twenty-one years.

Given Gunn's reputation as an 'official' portraitist, who could list royalty, aristocracy, eminent statesmen and leading figures in the world of the arts amongst his sitters, it is remarkable that so little critical material exists on his work. From what scant literature there is – interviews in his studio, biographical notes and obituaries – it is evident that *Conversation Piece* was perceived as a key work in Gunn's career. He exhibited it again, first in 1933 at the Royal Glasgow Institute[4] and then at his one-man exhibition at Barbizon House, London in 1935. It was also included in the memorial exhibition of his work mounted within the summer exhibition of the Royal Academy in 1965.[5] With its careful observation of physiognomy, 'the use of casual poses and the introduction of characteristic background',[6] Gunn's approach to subsequent group and individual portraits, such as *A Meeting of the Society of Dilettanti* (cat. 69) and *Delius* (cat. 53, plate 16) was established. Indeed, these two latter aspects of his portrait procedure were discussed by Gunn himself in some undated notes penned for a television company considering a programme on portrait painting. In these he stressed the importance of making a sitter, often unknown to him, relax, leaving him to 'more or less arrange himself', rather than be posed by the painter.

Striking though *Conversation Piece* certainly was to its audience in 1932, it did have direct prototypes in recent British portrait painting, most notably William Orpen's *Homage to Manet* (1909; Manchester City Art Gallery) and Henry Tonks's *Saturday Night in the Vale* (1929; bequeathed by William Orpen to the Tate Gallery, London). The former group portrait shows George Moore declaiming to the painters Steer, Tonks and Sickert, the critic D. S. MacColl and the collector Sir Hugh Lane, under Manet's portrait of Eva Gonzales which hung in Lane's Chelsea house. Tonks's work, painted at the request of Orpen, likewise represents George Moore, also declaiming, this time in Tonks's own studio at the Vale, Chelsea, to a group of friends: the St John Hutchinsons, the artist himself and Wilson Steer, who had dozed off. While all three conversation pieces celebrate leading figures in the fields of art and letters, presenting them informally in characteristic contexts, Gunn's work remains stylistically somewhat apart from the other two. Both Orpen and Tonks sought to impose a pictorial unity upon the individual constituent parts of their compositions, largely through the broad handling of brushwork. Gunn, in contrast, persisted in an almost super-real representation of his sitters, stressing their unique individuality and isolation from each other.

While parallels were drawn between Gunn's early work and, most notably, that of William Orpen and Ambrose McEvoy, it is this distinction between the unified approach of Orpen and the sharp focus of *Conversation Piece*, which initially marked Gunn for praise. It guaranteed his acceptability to those groups of patrons who sought security in an objective record of themselves rather than an expressionistic or subjective rendering in an innovative style derived from the European avant garde. As such, Gunn found himself cast within the more conventional, indeed 'conservative', school of British portrait painters. This affiliation inevitably focuses upon current definitions of portraiture, and Gunn's own perception of the issues raised therein. Unlike his immediate predecessors in the genre, notably Sargent, Lavery, Orpen, McEvoy and Augustus John, who tended to translate their own individual responses to sitters at the expense of immediate physical verisimilitude, Gunn believed 'quite unashamedly that a portrait should live up to its name and be first a likeness, sympathetic for choice, of the subject.' He thus had little sympathy for 'the artist who takes refuge in the cliché: "that is how I see him"' since he has 'generally made a bad portrait although it is possible he may have made an otherwise good picture. This is poor comfort however to the next of kin, who are, not unnaturally, more concerned with their own views than with the purely aesthetic reactions of a stranger and of posterity.'[7] There is no role for distortion of form within this prescription. Such an attitude put Gunn firmly within the more 'traditionalist' camp, as he himself admitted: '[A portrait] must be traditional and sane, and is consequently a steadying force in times of revolt.' This concern to confront directly the appearance and character of his sitters set Gunn firmly against the avant garde in both London and Paris, as formulated in particular in Britain by Roger Fry and Herbert Read. Instead, it allied him philosophically, if not technically, to that apparently 'alternative' school of early twentieth-century British painting, led by Henry Tonks and enshrined in the practices of the Slade School of Art. Artist, co-author with George Clausen of *Elementary Propositions in Drawing and Painting* (1910), Professor of Drawing at the Slade School from 1918 to 1930 and a lifetime member of the New English Art Club, Tonks was best known for his public sparring with Roger Fry over the latter's championing of what Tonks perceived to be the iniquitous 'School of Cézanne', epitomised in the work of Picasso and Braque. Unable to accept the intrusion of a subjective vision which he held inevitably distorted form, Tonks adhered steadfastly to the central role of drawing as the basis of a sound art which was dependent upon objective observation. In a letter to Collins Baker of 2 November 1931, he declared in words very similar to those used by Gunn in relation to the demands of portraiture: 'All great painting, and possibly poetry too, is objective. The great change which has come over painting in my lifetime is the leaning towards subjectivity, a sure sign of decline.'[8]

Given the relatively conservative character of the Royal Academy during the first half of this century prior to Sir Gerald Kelly's more liberal presidency, ushered in after the resignation of Sir Alfred Munnings in 1949, Gunn's belief in the 'traditional' nature of portraiture should have found favour amongst its members and hence assured his early entry into that institution. Sir Arthur Cope's report of the members' admiration of *Conversation Piece* would appear to support such a contention. Yet Gunn did not become an Associate of the Royal Academy until 1953, when he was 59, ten years older than the average age of election, and he was only elected into full membership eight years after that. Such delayed entry to the Academy had little to do with his support for the institution itself, demonstrated most notably in his commitment to exhibiting at the annual summer exhibitions. From his first presentation of two works in 1923[9] until his death in 1964, he had 133 works accepted and hung. In his memorial presentation shown in the summer exhibition of 1965, six works were included, of which five were finished portraits: *Conversation Piece* (cat. 47, plate 15), *Delius* (cat. 53, plate 16) *James Pryde* and *Father Vincent McNab*,[10] which hung together, and a portrait of his wife Pauline (cat. 59, plate 19)[11] and a landscape[12] which were placed elsewhere in the galleries. Usually, he achieved an entry of three works per annum, the maximum number of works permitted to a non-member of the Royal Academy for inclusion in any one exhibition, with the exception of 1944 and 1945, when non-members were permitted to submit and have hung an additional work; Gunn partook of this exceptional ruling, having four portraits accepted and hung in each year. In terms of subject matter, it would appear that only six of the 133 works were landscapes, the remaining 127 works being portraits. Gunn was thus clearly identifying himself as a portraitist within this public domain. In addition, apart from *Conversation Piece*, which was accorded the status[13] of 'picture of the year' when shown in 1932, his portrait of the ailing composer, Delius, shown in the following year, was also accorded this status, as was *Pauline in the Yellow Dress* (cat. 58, plate 18) when hung in the summer exhibition of 1944.

Yet progress at the Royal Academy's summer exhibitions was not without its intermittent and painful setbacks. Twice Gunn had the ignominious experience of having

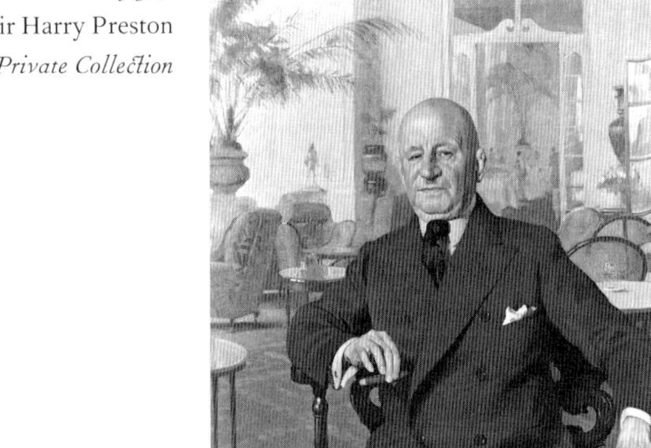

his work wholly rejected by the Academy's selection committee, first in 1935, and then in 1942. That he saw those rejections as major rebukes delivered by the institution can be seen not only in his sending, and having accepted, in 1935, two portraits to the Royal Glasgow Institute's annual exhibition[14] and another portrait, *My Wife*, to the Royal Scottish Academy's summer exhibition,[15] but also in his arranging a one-man exhibition at Knoedler's Gallery, London in July of the same year. This exhibition included the publicly acclaimed works of the preceding two Royal Academy summer exhibitions, *Conversation Piece* and *Delius* and the recently rejected portrait, *Sir Harry Preston* (fig. 9). Knoedler's catalogue included a preface provided by Hilaire Belloc himself. In 1942, rather than resorting to outside exhibitions to make his point, Gunn penned, but probably did not in the end send, a pained letter to the then President of the Royal Academy, the architect, Sir Edwin Lutyens. Deploring the fact that he had 'suffered the complete rejection of my work by your great institution', he declared that 'it is a grievous and humiliating experience', but determined 'such a thing will never happen again'.

Was the fact that Gunn had experienced two outright rejections by the Academy's selection committee a possible reason for his delayed election to its membership? That it was delayed there can be little doubt. Of the twenty-eight painter members who, like Gunn, had been born within the decade of the 1890s, nineteen were elected Associate members of the Royal Academy before Gunn, and twenty achieved full Academician status before his election in 1961. Of the nineteen who preceded him to Associate membership, some were working in the same objective, realist style as Gunn. These included Gerald Brockhurst (ARA 1928, RA 1937) and Meredith Frampton (ARA 1932, RA 1942). As regards the immediate preceding generation of members, Gunn's work should logically have found support within the lineage of such recently deceased Royal Academicians as Charles Sims (died 1928) and William Strang (died 1921), as well as from Orpen, McEvoy and, most particularly, the future President, Sir Gerald Kelly. In addition, as an adherent of Tonks's commitment to objective observation as the fundamental principle underlying quality in art, Gunn could also presumably have found favour with those artists such as George Clausen and Walter Russell who had joined the Royal Academy in 1895 and 1920 respectively from earlier affiliations with Tonks at the New English Art Club and the Slade School of Art.

Gunn's ultimate election to the Royal Academy may well have been activated by the then President, Sir Gerald Kelly (1949–1954), for the two men evidently shared a very similar approach to portraiture. Both adopted the same objective rendering of their sitters and both used their wives regularly as subjects. However, when Associateship did arrive, Gunn appears to have been less than excited. In his notes prepared for a speech delivered in Glasgow in 1955, he declared: 'The Royal Academy came two years ago when it meant little'. Yet, despite pressure from certain quarters not to accept this honour, and perhaps with the spectre of the two rejections of 1935 and 1942 still haunting his memory, he accepted, admitting that 'at last I could send my work with the certainty that only flagrant indecency would prevent acceptance'. In the end, his attitude towards the Royal Academy was perhaps encapsulated in his obvious admiration for the institution as the repository of the great names in British art, Sir Joshua Reynolds and Thomas Gainsborough: 'After all, it is the Queen's Academy. It is Sir Joshua, Gainsborough and all the shining names that light its history, and who am I to refuse to be remembered amongst these'.[17]

In this respect Gunn was reflecting a set of artistic standards enshrined in the eighteenth century which he shared with several of his contemporaries – not those of the more radical persuasion, but rather those who believed in an intrinsically English tradition. These standards had been upheld by Lavery, Wilson Steer and Augustus John, and advocated in such texts as Frank Rutter's *Modern Masterpieces*, published in the 1930s. Rutter had included among 'portrait painters of the new century', Sargent, G. W. Furse, Robert Brough, William Orpen and Ambrose McEvoy; and his list of 'some leaders of British Painting' included James Pryde, Henry Tonks and Wilson Steer. It was to the traditions represented by these painters that James Gunn subscribed and in the context of whose work his own painting should still be seen.

1. No. 430.

2. Vaughan Dryden, 'Celebrities in the Studio' (article in untraced journal).

3. Biographical notes made for a speech delivered to Glasgow Art Club, 18 November 1955.

4. No. 178; he also showed a portrait of Sir Iain Colquhoun, no. 501.

5. No. 151.

6. Sybil Vincent, 'In the Studio of James Gunn', *The Studio*, December 1936, pp. 319–21.

7. Sybil Vincent *op. cit.*, p. 319.

8. C. H. Collins Baker, 'Tonks as an Artist', in Joseph Hone, *The Life of Henry Tonks*, London and Toronto, 1939, p. 347.

9. *The Pink Coats*, no. 638, and *The Doulton Chimney*, no. 644.

10. Nos. 151, 153, 154 and 155 respectively.

11. No. 336.

12. *St Paul de Vence*, no. 799.

13. According to Sidney Hutchison, *The History of the Royal Academy*, pp. 172–3

14. *John Drummond Jr* DL, ex-Provost of Greenock, no. 408, and *My Family*, no. 452.

15. No. 327.

16. Ms Gunn Collection. The letter and envelope, fully addressed, survive, giving rise to the suggestion that the letter had been written but possibly never posted. No copy survives in the Royal Academy Archives.

17. Biographical notes made for a speech delivered to Glasgow Art Club, 18 November 1955.

A MEMOIR

IN THE first eleven years of their marriage my parents moved at least eight times. Their speciality was buying up the last months of leases at progressively grander addresses until in 1939, Hyde Park Street having come to an end, they were negotiating for a house in the corner of Orme Square. The outbreak of war deflected them from this, and we went instead to a furnished house in East Grinstead. There my father and my mother's brother Guy, a soldier on leave at the time, excavated a tomb-like shelter in the paddock. They camouflaged it, lined it with boards and dug out a little niche for first aid equipment. I don't think we had much use of it, even as a place to play, for it rapidly began to fill with water.

We were soon on the move again: a commission to paint Mr Robson, the Town Clerk of Dumfries, changed our lives. We were taken along, for a holiday, and were staying at the Cairndale Hotel when the first bombs dropped on London. My father returned to Pembroke Walk, and left my mother with my brother Paul and me in Dumfries. He had not been accepted as a war artist and thought the proffered job in the Camouflage Corps a poor substitute, so he became an air raid warden. After seven months in the hotel, my mother found a little house out on the Solway Firth and took a 7–14–21 year lease. We kept that house until after her death, and lived there for very much longer than we had ever lived anywhere in London. The house they had wanted to live in in Orme Square received a direct hit during the blitz.

I was born at 17 John Street, Adelphi, London. There was no room anywhere in the flat for my pram, and it was checked in every night at the left luggage at Charing Cross Station. Though I knew nothing of their existence until I was eleven, my father already had three daughters by his marriage to Gwen. This had ended in divorce in 1927. Thereafter he saw almost nothing of the three children, Diana, Elizabeth and Pauline, until they were grown up, and came to see him of their own accord. Elizabeth remembers him dashing up the stairs of 38 Lansdowne Road, while his family were still living there, and giving her a chocolate rabbit. She ate it, and then bitterly regretted so doing, as she was left without the thing he had given her. On another occasion in 1929 he was working on a mural for Turner Layton and went to the zoo to make some animal studies. There, by the lion house, he chanced to meet all three children with their nurse. He wrote to my mother, who before they married was working at Elizabeth Arden in Rome, telling her how he had been chided by Diana for not loving them very much, for he was always too busy to come to see them. For him it was all too painful, and we were never told of his first marriage until, on a visit with my mother to a friend working in the American Embassy, I was found with a *Who's Who*, searching for the entry which in our copy had a large lump out of the very page to which we would naturally turn. It was seized from me, and on returning home I was given the astonishing information that I had three half-sisters. My father never talked to us of Gwen or his first family until we were grown up, though my aunt Sylvia was less restrained, and of course we were fascinated by her recollections.

It is hard to reconcile the father we knew with the young man who left the close-knit life of a large family in Glasgow to go with twenty golden guineas in a pouch to Paris in 1911 – a lonely eighteen-year old whose companions seem for the most part to have been other students from Edinburgh. He wrote almost daily postcards home full of the small details of life, the weather, the model at Julian's, the 'preach' at the Scots kirk,

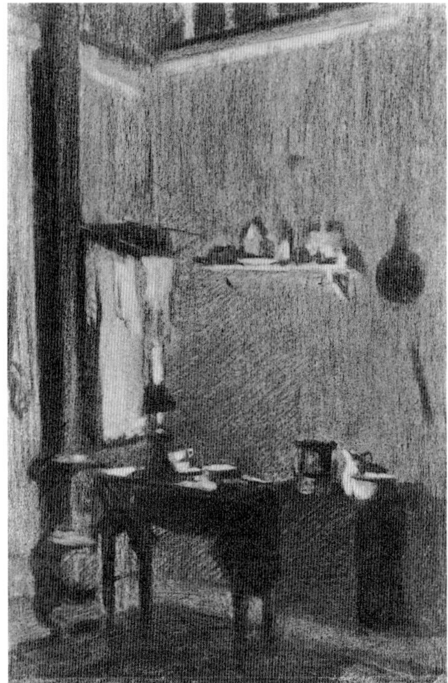

what he had seen at the Louvre on a wet day. A little charcoal drawing of a corner of his room at 2 bis rue Perrel survives. It must have been done by the light of an oil lamp which sits on the small table with a few bits of crockery. A frying pan hangs on the wall, and the chimney of a great cast-iron stove dominates the scene (cat. 3, fig. 10). A love of Paris remained with him all his life: we heard tales of the old woman who sold *frites* from a hole in the wall, and would cook his piece of meat in the boiling oil, of a shared overcoat so that he and the sculptor Harry Paulin took it in turns to go out, and most exciting of all, of being taken to meet Rodin. With a sculpture student of Percy Portsmouth's from Edinburgh, Nathandra Bose, he was introduced to the great man by a Polish countess. One Sunday Rodin told Bose to do a head of his companion, *'pas plus grand que ça'* he said with thumb and finger outstretched. When the head was delivered to Rodin the verdict was that this young man had nothing to learn. Bose went home, having borrowed quite a few of the golden guineas and within months he was dead of tuberculosis. The head disappeared until 1947 when the plaster turned up in Portsmouth's studio. It was cast in bronze and came by post to the house at Kidderpore Avenue. Someone must have thought it was the packet of often rancid butter sent each week by an aunt worried about my mother's health. It was put straight into the fridge, and the revelation, weeks later, of what was in the heavy brown package was an occasion of much merriment.

There was another subject too painful to be talked about, and that was the '14–18' war. It only came home to me fully when, in the 1950s, I took my father to see Joan Littlewood's *Oh, What a Lovely War!*, and caught a sideways glance of his expression as we sat in the theatre. The last three of Richard and Thomasina Gunn's ten children were boys: Stanley, Herbert, as my father was then known, and the youngest, Charles. Stanley was wounded and died in France in 1915, and Charles, my father's great companion, the subject of some of his very early portraits, the correspondent, friend and admirer, who had printed his etchings, listed his pictures and always looked after him, was twenty-one when he was killed in 1917. The two brothers had agreed to try and let each other know if one of them 'got it'. At five one morning my father started from sleep, waking his companions, who were none too pleased at being disturbed, to say that he knew that Charles was dead. Two days later came the confirmation.

The self-portraits which he did over the years, the evolution of his signature as by stages he abandoned Herbert for James, tell their own story. In the end it was Lord Lee of Fareham who urged him to cut out the H. and call himself James Gunn. His friends all called him Jimmy, and only his brothers and sisters persisted with Heb, a name which he claimed to detest.

As with Gwen and her children, my mother, my brother and I were frequently called upon to sit. I remember the stream of conversation designed to stop us from yawning (to do so was the eighth deadly sin). He talked to all his sitters and they to him. We could not compete with the interest he derived from all these people who came, morning and afternoon, to sit on the throne. There were lots of chairs in the studio – he collected them to suit various shapes and sizes – and I still have a pretty yellow *bergère* bought especially for the Queen Mother.

Writing again to Pauline in Rome in 1929, when they were hesitating to marry for lack of funds, he said, 'If I was full of work I would be happy and could keep going daily from 10 till 6 like the working man. Please God that condition comes soon.' It did, and he did, to within three weeks of his death, not only Monday to Friday, but weekends too, and on holiday, when, as relief from faces, he reverted to landscape painting while we went off to the beach.

We went occasionally to the studio in Bedford Gardens and later on, Pembroke Walk. Our birthday parties took place in those vast rather airless rooms redolent of turpentine. One awful morning I woke up with chicken-pox and had to stay at home imagining the goings on at my own party.

Then there was Angela, a comfortable kind woman who was his secretary. She seemed to have been there always, but probably took on the job of factotum when he first separated from Gwen and went to live in the Bedford Gardens studio. She ran his life in a somewhat haphazard fashion, and had on her desk a heavy and ever growing ball made from the silver paper wrappings of her many cigarettes. During the war, when we had no home in London, we spent occasional nights at Pembroke Walk. Not being allowed to sleep under the great north-facing skylights, we had mattresses in the little entrance hall or, much worse, were put to sleep in the claustrophobic Anderson shelter which had been installed in the box room.

Looking back there seems to have been a real dichotomy in our way of life: in some ways it was very conventional and in others quite unlike that of anyone else we knew. There was a secretary at the studio, nursemaids and cooks at home, my father always wore a suit and tie, and exchanged the jacket for a blue or white overall when he started work. (The truth is, he had too many suits, for his surviving older brothers who had been obliged to continue in the family tailoring business in Glasgow, instead of pursuing wished-for careers in medicine and music, were always saying they had a nice piece of material, and sending down boxes of clothes which never truly fitted.) By 1937 we had quite an establishment: Mitzi, the Austrian cook, her sister Grethel, the housemaid, and Elizabeth, our beloved German governess who stayed with us from 1934 until she went on holiday in August 1939. She taught me what she knew, so I spoke fluent German, and after she had gone my parents realised that I could only write *schrift*, that Gothic German script. I was subjected to some pretty vigorous re-education before I could be sent away to school. We did not see Elizabeth again until 1946 when my father persuaded one of his sitters, who was in a position to do so, to get her a permit to visit us. She arrived at Carsethorn on the Solway Firth for an emotional reunion. We had spent the greater part of the war there, doing the most

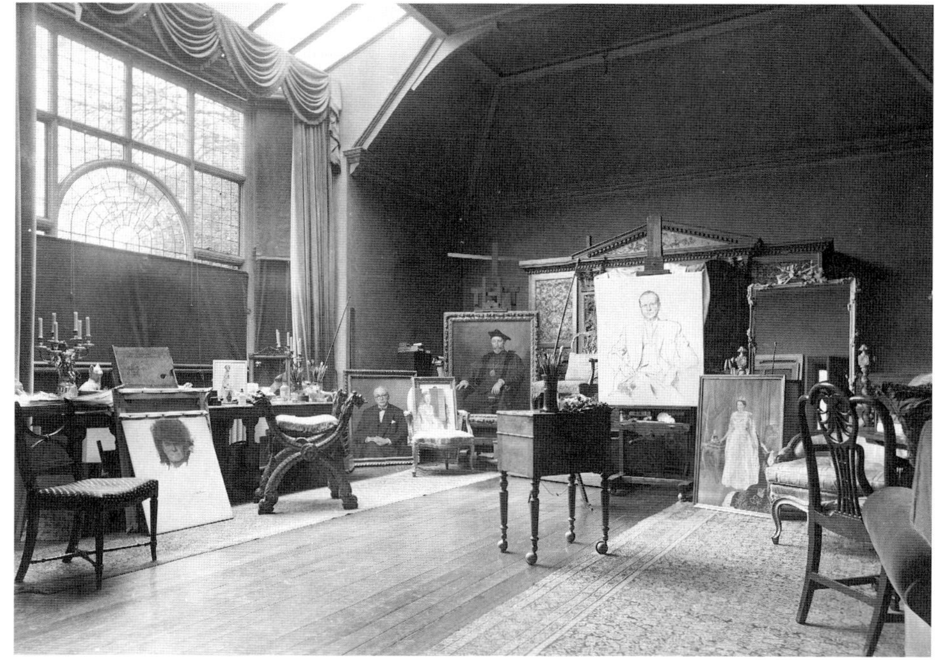

fig. 11
The artist's studio,
Kidderpore Avenue
*c.*1955

undisciplined lessons with another governess in the bar parlour of the Steamboat Inn.

The years after the war were sad ones: my mother had cancer and went through much pain and many operations. The devotion of my father was extraordinary. When they moved to Kidderpore Avenue, the only property they ever owned, for the first time the studio and the house were adjoining (fig. 11). This allowed them to see much more of each other. His care of her was exemplary, as though he was making an enormous effort to make up for past deficiencies. He worked in the daytime, and continued to paint her, poignant images, hard to contemplate even now. Until a few days before her death in September 1950, he nursed her every night, summoned from sleep by a little buzzer. It wore him out, and only later did he confess that he had begun, due to the stress and fatigue, to suffer from double vision.

In October, two weeks after my mother's death, I was due to go up to Oxford. I never thought I would be able to, but my father insisted that he would be all right and that I should go. He drove me to Somerville in his reckless fashion. He was a terrible driver who prided himself on an acute sense of distance, but he had had a number of accidents, and had frightened many a passenger with his fine judgements.

He survived my mother by thirteen years. As far as his work was concerned, she had been not only the subject of many of his most memorable pictures but she had always been allowed to criticise and comment, and he took notice of what she said. No one else was ever able to do this for him. His portraits continued to be much in demand and he found consolation in work. We came and went. A wonderful Irish house keeper, Kate, kept everything going. He dined out most nights, invited by friends or dropping in to the Garrick, the Savage or the Beefsteak, and he particularly enjoyed evenings spent at Grillons and the Dilettanti. He painted his grandchildren, forcing them into momentary attention with such teases as 'Baa Baa green sheep', and his last picture, which we found signed on the easel after he had gone into hospital, was of his eighteen-month old granddaughter, Oriana (fig. 12).

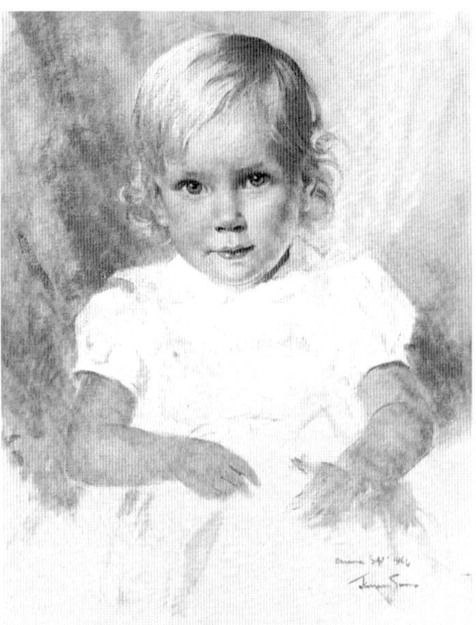

fig. 12
Oriana
Private Collection
The artist's last
picture

CHRONOLOGY

1893

30 June, Herbert James Gunn born at 56 Wilton Street, Glasgow, ninth of the ten children of Richard Gunn, a tailor, and Thomasina, née Munro. Richard Gunn was a staunch member of the United Free Church of Scotland, in the parish of George Reith, father of Lord Reith. He was also an unremitting campaigner against Free Trade. He wrote a book on the subject, *The Social Trinity*, illustrated by his son Herbert in 1908.

1898

Attended drawing lessons with A. Brownlie Docharty, a family friend.

1902–8

Educated at Glasgow High School. In 1904 and 1906 won prizes from the Corporation of Glasgow Museums and Art Galleries for his drawings of natural history objects and museum specimens. Family holidays were spent at Lochearnhead where some of his earliest landscapes were painted.

1908

Taken to London by his father where they visited the President of the Royal Academy, Sir Edward Poynter and the Keeper, Sir Arthur Cope. It was suggested that he should enrol in the Royal Academy Schools but, back in Scotland, another and more local connection, the engraver Clouston Young, advised his father to send him to Edinburgh College of Art.

1909

Against this advice, began his training at Glasgow School of Art, but this was short lived due to his lack of sympathy with the school's head, Maurice Greiffenhagen. His father sent him to work as a commercial artist in an office where he designed lids for biscuit tins. Exhibited *Halloween*, a portrait of his brother Charles by lamplight, at the Royal Glasgow Institute of the Fine Arts. It was sold for £7.

1910–11

Enrolled at Edinburgh College of Art, then directed by Morley Fletcher. Was taught etching by Ernest Lumsden and formed a lasting friendship with the head of sculpture, Percy Portsmouth. Met and formed a life-long friendship with the painter W. O. Hutchison.

1911–12

Moved to Paris where he took a room at 2 bis rue Perrel and enrolled at the Académie Julian under Jean-Paul Laurens. Began to paint around the city, mostly on small boards, and made regular visits to the Louvre to draw from the old masters.

1912–13

Returned to live at 24 York Place, Edinburgh, but spent some time in London and made a number of etchings for the art dealer, Dowdeswell.

1913

Exhibited his first two portraits at the Royal
Scottish Academy.

1914

March-June at the instigation of the London
dealer, W. B. Paterson, travelled widely in
Spain and visited Tangier and Gibraltar. Sent
parcels of pictures home to Scotland which his
brother Charles collected at the docks.
Returned home via Paris and Etretat to a
studio at 16 Newton Terrace, Glasgow, rented
for him by his father while he was away. Began
to use the signature H. J. Gunn in place of
Herbert or simply H. Gunn.

1915

In September, stayed with the Patersons in
Warwick Avenue, London and sketched at
Kew, Richmond and on Hampstead Heath.
Enlisted in the Artists' Rifles. His brother
Stanley was killed on active service, near
Givenchy.

1916

Stationed in Northern France where for a
short time he had his own studio in the
barracks.

1917

Commissioned into the 10th Battalion Scottish
Rifles. His drawings of fellow officers were
later published in a book, *The 10th Battalion,
The Cameronians (Scottish Rifles): a Record and
a Memorial 1914–1918*. His brother Charles
was killed in action aged 21.

1918

Stationed at Invergordon where he met
Gwendoline Thorne. On 24 March he received
his demobilisation notice. On 31 December his
father, Richard Gunn, died after a long illness.

1919

On 9 January married Gwendoline Charlotte
Thorne, née Hillman, widow of Captain G. S.
Thorne, Royal Flying Corps (brought down
near Arras in March 1917). They left Glasgow
to stay at Marazion in Cornwall. In June had a
one-man exhibition at W. B. Paterson's in Old
Bond Street and in December at T. & R.
Annan & Sons in Glasgow.

1920

Lived at Rookwood, Chadlington near
Oxford. Exhibited in November with T. & R.
Annan & Sons.

1921

Designed magazine covers for *Open Air*, *Out of
Doors* and worked for *The Illustrated Sporting
and Dramatic News*. Continued to exhibit at the
Royal Glasgow Institute and in London.
Exhibited at the Grosvenor Gallery alongside
Sir John Lavery and William Rothenstein. In
January his first child, Diana Mary, was born.

1922

A second daughter, Anne Elizabeth, was born
in July.

1923

Had his first painting accepted by the Royal
Academy in London. Pauline, his third
daughter, was born in December.

1924

His first portrait of James Pryde was exhibited
at the Royal Glasgow Institute and sold for
£450 to the Scottish Modern Arts Association.
A drawing of Sir John Lavery RA, was shown
at the Royal Academy in London.

1925

Moved to London and rented 38 Lansdowne Road. Exhibited a self-portrait at the Royal Scottish Academy. Owing to lung trouble, sustained in the war when he was gassed, took a cruise to Argentina, going out on the *Arlanza*, returning immediately on the *Andes*. Whilst on board, painted several pictures of other passengers.

1926

Went to live in his studio at 12 Bedford Gardens. Belonged to the Savage and Beefsteak Clubs, and found many subjects among his fellow members. Travelled to Antibes and returned via Paris. He changed his signature from H. J. Gunn to H. James Gunn.

1927

Exhibited at Colnaghi & Co., *Portraits and Landscapes by H. J. Gunn*. A portrait of his friend W. O. Hutchison was shown at the Royal Scottish Academy. His divorce from Gwen was made absolute.

1928–9

December to January, went to visit Pauline Miller, then working in Rome, and exhibited the first of many portraits of her at *The Spring Exhibition of Modern Painters*, Southport Art Galleries.

1929

Exhibited at The Fine Art Society, *Paintings of Rome etc. by H. J. Gunn*. Portraits of Hilaire Belloc and Charles Pond were shown at the Royal Academy, London. Married Marie Pauline Miller on 22 August in Paris. Set up home in Adelphi Terrace, London.

1930

Moved around the corner to 17 John Street, Adelphi. Exhibited *Pauline, Wife of the Artist* at the Royal Academy and painted George Balfour of Balfour Beatty, who became his most important patron. *Conversation Piece*, a portrait of Belloc, Chesterton and Baring, was instigated at a dinner party to celebrate Belloc's 60th birthday. Chloë Marya was born in December.

1932

Exhibited *Conversation Piece* at the Royal Academy. It was sold to George Balfour for £1,500 before the official opening. Exhibited his second portrait of James Pryde at the Royal Society of Portrait Painters. Travelled to Grez-sur-Loing in France to paint the aged, blind and paralysed composer, Delius.

1933

Delius was exhibited at the Royal Academy and given pride of place in the centre gallery. It was bought for £1,250 by George Balfour. Exhibited *London Pictures and Recent Portraits* at Barbizon House. Omitted the H from his signature and began to sign his pictures James Gunn.

1934

A third portrait of James Pryde was shown at the Royal Academy. A son, Paul Munro, was born in April.

1935

Moved his studio to 3 Pembroke Walk, London. All his paintings were rejected by the Royal Academy. Seemingly in response, he held a one-man show of sixteen paintings at Knoedler's, Old Bond Street. In March, he exhibited with C. R. W. Nevinson and James Pryde at T. & R. Annan & Sons in Glasgow.

In 1935-6 went to work in Paris. He and his family lived at 18 Quai d'Orléans. Exhibited *Pauline in Paris* at the Royal Academy and the Royal Glasgow Institute.

1938
Painted the Prime Minister, The Rt Hon Neville Chamberlain, for the Carlton Club. 30,000 readers of the *Rochdale Observer* subscribed one shilling to a fund established to pay for a portrait of Gracie Fields.

1939
Received a Gold Medal from the Salon, Paris, for *My Studio and Myself*.

1940
Pauline Waiting shown at the Royal Scottish Academy and *Gracie Fields* at the Royal Academy.

1942
For the first time since 1935, had nothing accepted by the Royal Academy.

1944
Between 28 August and 19 September travelled from Falaise to Brussels in the caravan next to Field-Marshal Montgomery, painting his portrait. Exhibited portraits *Field-Marshal Sir Bernard Montgomery in Battle Dress* and *HM King George VI* at the Royal Academy. Another portrait of his wife, *Pauline in the Yellow Dress*, was voted picture of the year. Awarded an honorary degree of Doctor of Law by Manchester University.

1945
The *Sunday Dispatch* bought a second, less formal, portrait of Field-Marshal Montgomery for Montgomery's mother. It was exhibited at the Royal Academy along with a small picture, *Field-Marshal Montgomery with his personal staff in the mess-tent* and another portrait of his wife, *Pauline: Venetian Souvenir*. Elected a member of the Royal Society of Portrait Painters.

1946
Exhibited *Her Majesty Queen Elizabeth* at the Royal Academy and had an exhibition *First Impressions* at Thomas Agnew & Sons, Old Bond Street, London.

1947
Moved to 7 Kidderpore Avenue, Hampstead. Exhibited *Sir William Y. Darling* at the Royal Academy.

1949
Experimented with the palette knife and painted a number of small landscapes at Mougins.

1950
Exhibited *Hilaire Belloc, King's Land*, painted for the Oxford Union, and *Conversation Piece at Royal Lodge Windsor* at the Royal Academy. *The Rt Hon C. R. Attlee CH, MP* was shown at the Royal Society of Portrait Painters. On 22 September his wife Pauline died.

1951
Became a member of Grillons and the Society of Dilettanti.

1952
Exhibited the portrait *W. O. Hutchison dressed in the robes and chain of office of the President of the Royal Scottish Academy*, at the Royal Academy.

1953
The portrait *Her Majesty, Queen Elizabeth II*, commissioned by the Royal Artillery Regiment, exhibited at the Royal Academy. It was voted portrait of the year. Appointed President of the Royal Society of Portrait Painters on his 60th birthday. On 3 April, finally elected an Associate member of the Royal Academy. Became the honorary secretary to the Artists' General Benevolent Institution. In September, began work at Balmoral on the Coronation State Portrait, *Her Majesty The Queen*.

1954
The Coronation State Portrait was exhibited at the Royal Academy.

1957
Became Chairman of the Artists' General Benevolent Institution.

1958
Accepted an unusual invitation to become an Honorary Texan along with Sir Winston Churchill, Lord Beaverbrook and Graham Greene.

1959
Painted the large group portrait, *The Society of Dilettanti*.

1960
Commissioned by the Carlton Club to paint the Prime Minister, Harold Macmillan.

1961
21 February elected to full membership of the Royal Academy at the General Assembly. *Pauline Waiting* was deposited as his diploma work on his election as an Academician.

1962
A second portrait of Macmillan was commissioned by former Balliol men in Parliament.

1963
Received a knighthood in the New Year's Honours and an honorary degree from the University of Glasgow.

1964
Invited to succeed Sir Basil Spence as Treasurer of the Royal Academy but died before taking office on 30 December at the age of 71.

1965
The Royal Academy exhibited a memorial group of his paintings which included *Father Vincent McNab*, *Conversation Piece*, *James Pryde*, *Delius* and *Pauline: Venetian Souvenir*.

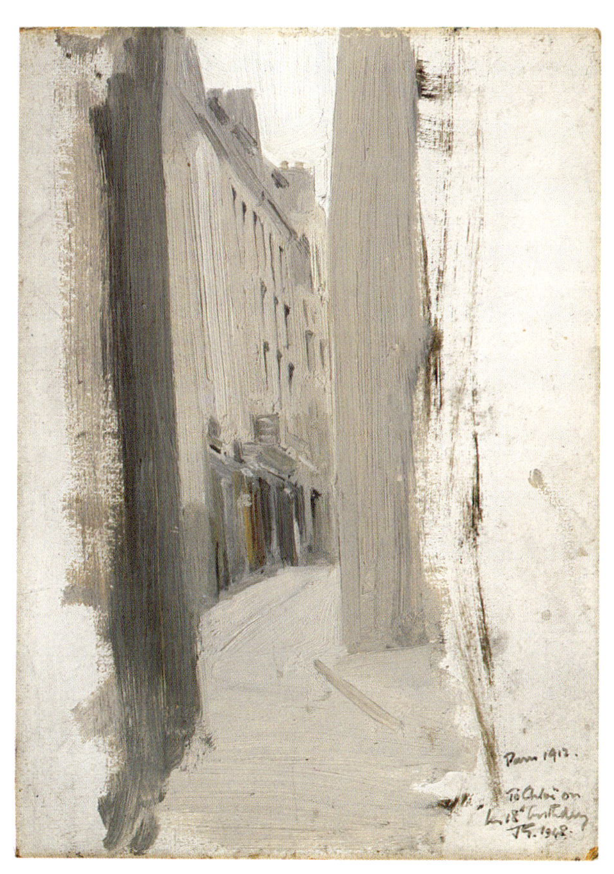

PLATE I

RUE DE NEVERS, PARIS

1912, CAT. 6

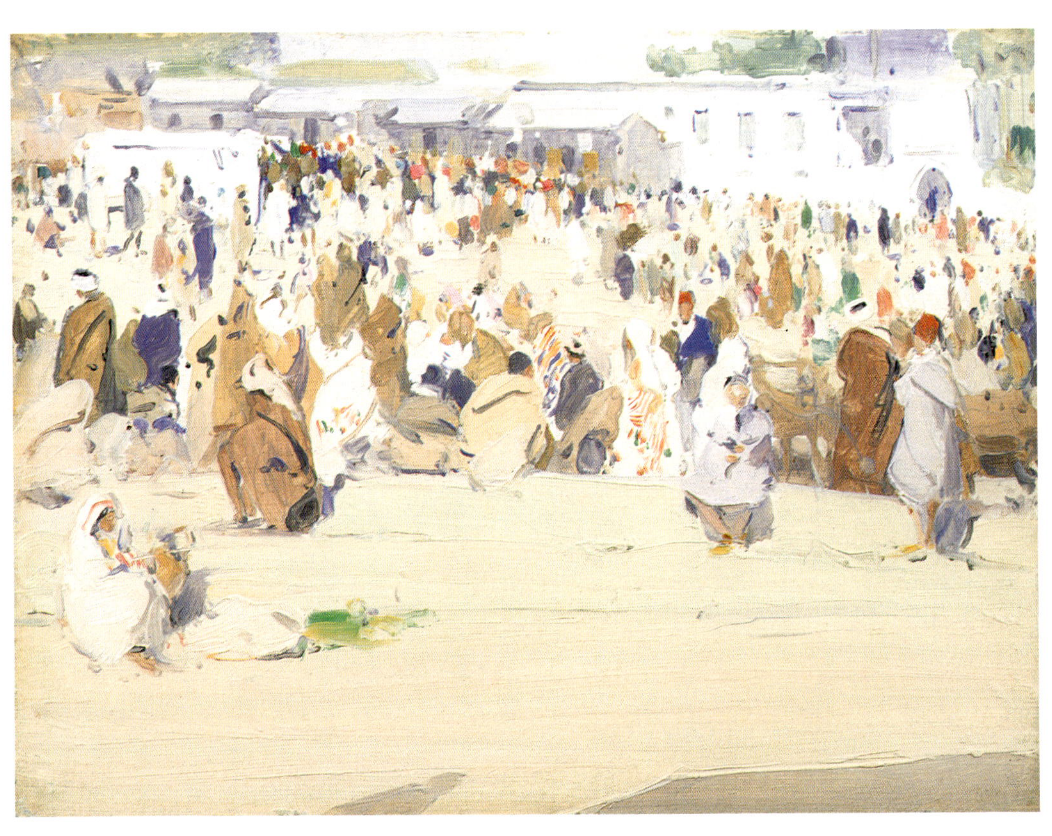

PLATE 2

THE SOCCO, TANGIER

1914, CAT. 13

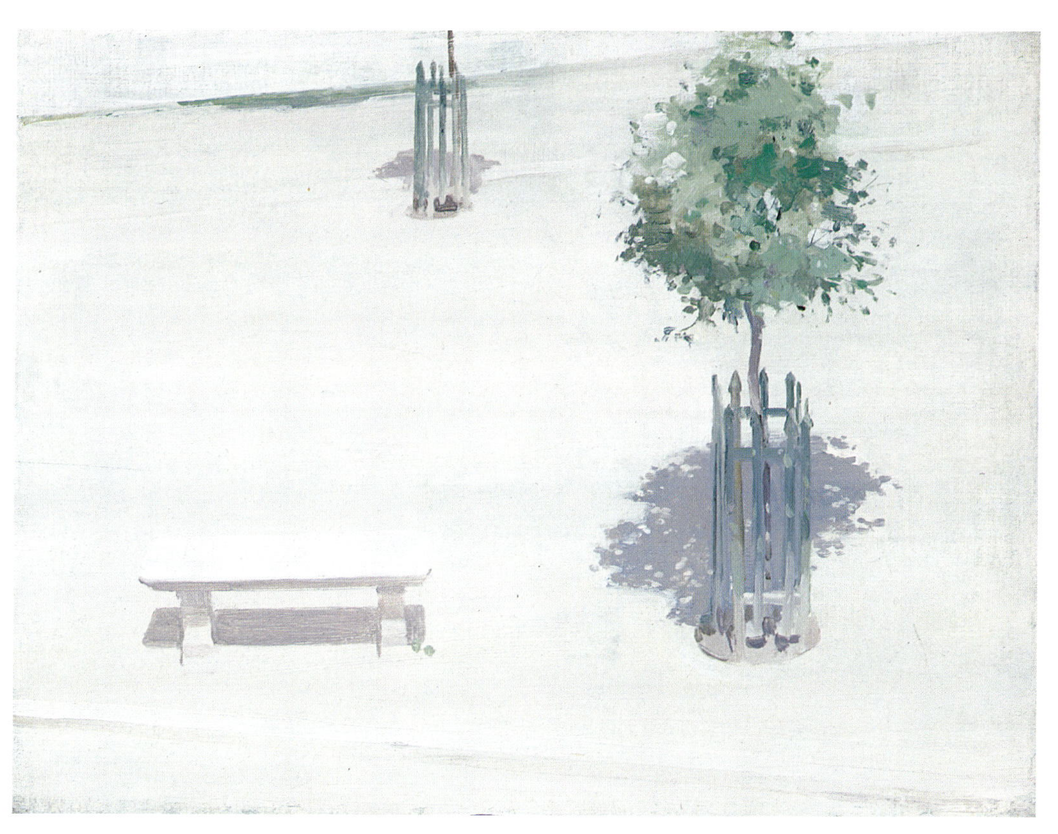

PLATE 3
FROM MY WINDOW, RONDA
1914, CAT. 15

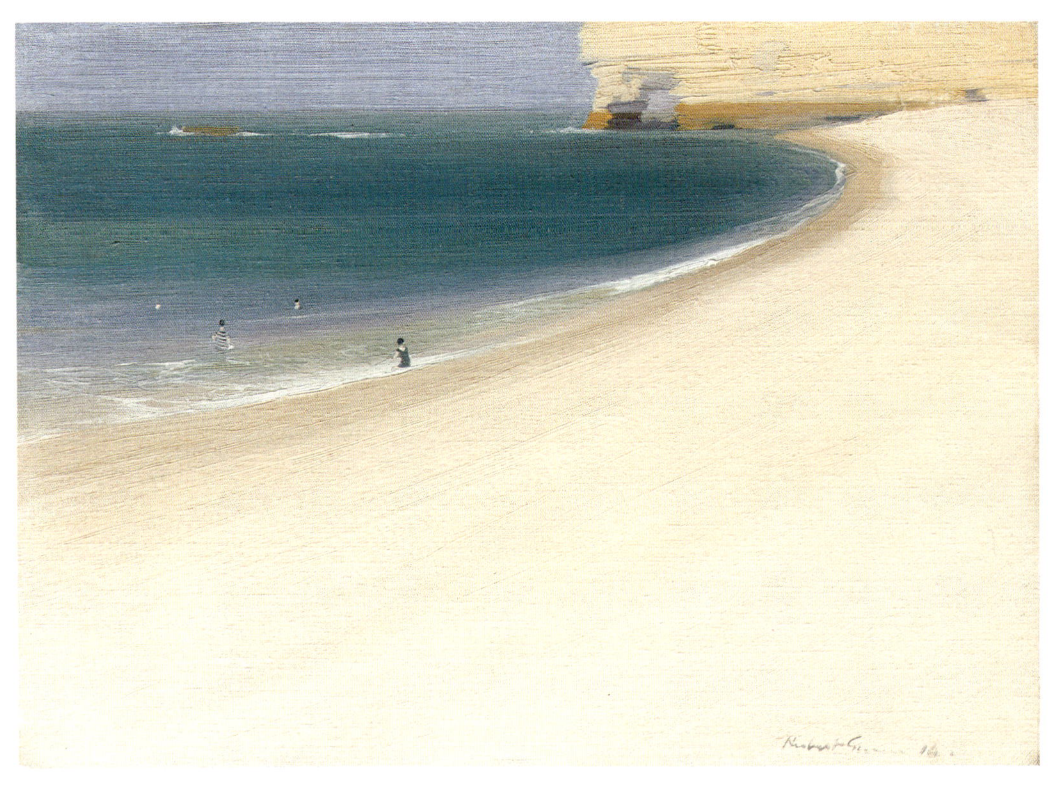

PLATE 4

ETRETAT

1914, CAT. 19

PLATE 5
LA PLAGE, ETRETAT
1914, CAT. 20

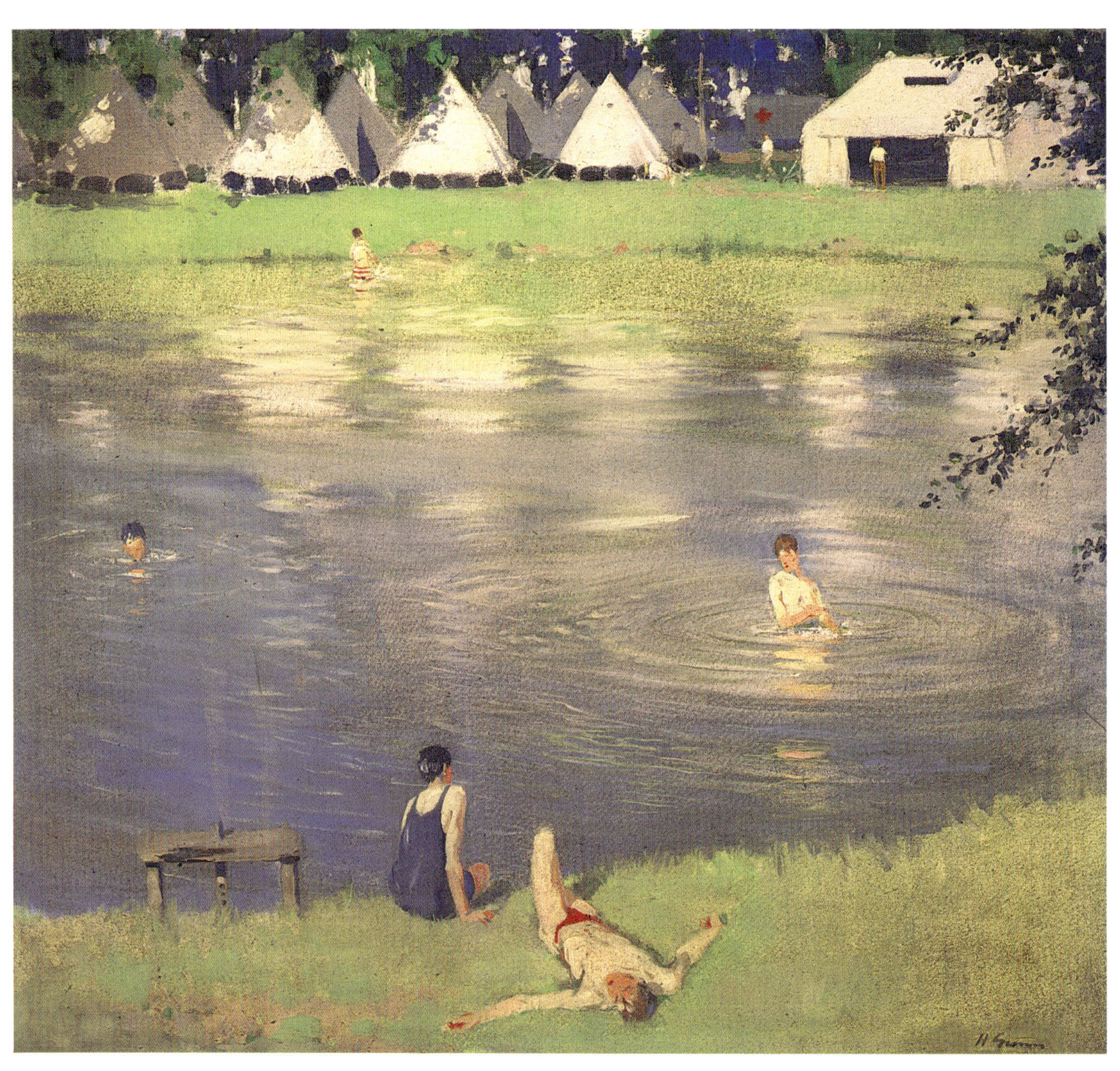

PLATE 6

THE EVE OF THE BATTLE OF THE SOMME

1916, CAT. 21

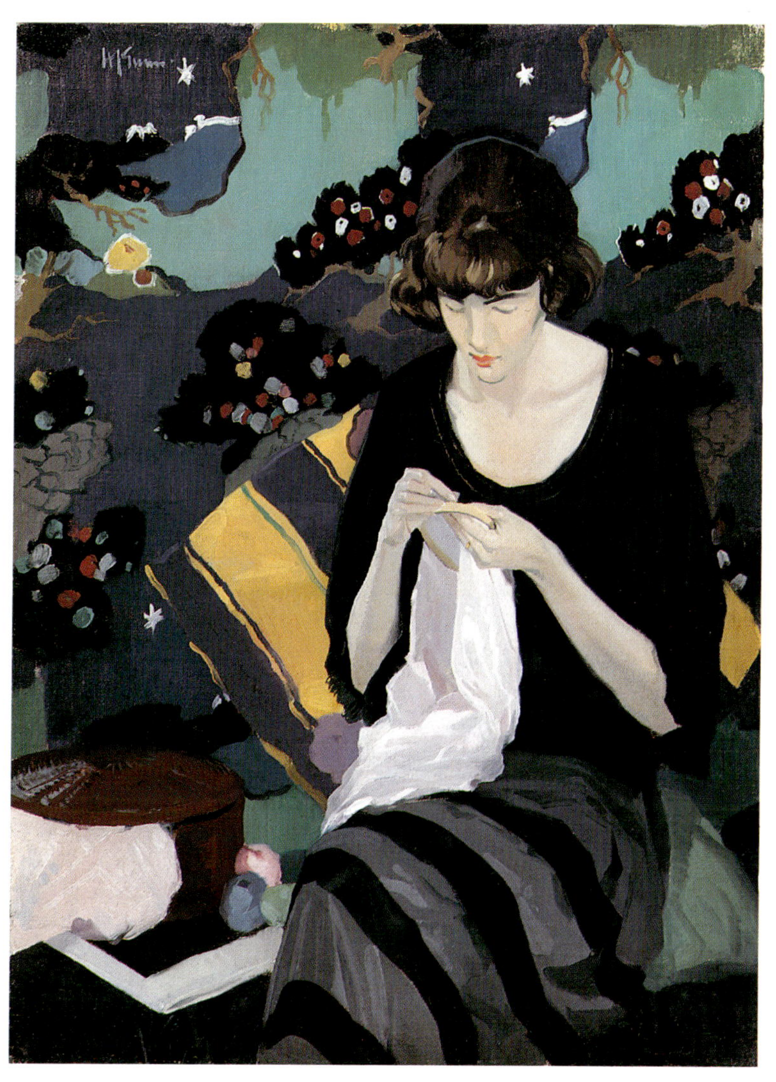

PLATE 7

GWEN SEWING

c.1920, CAT. 25

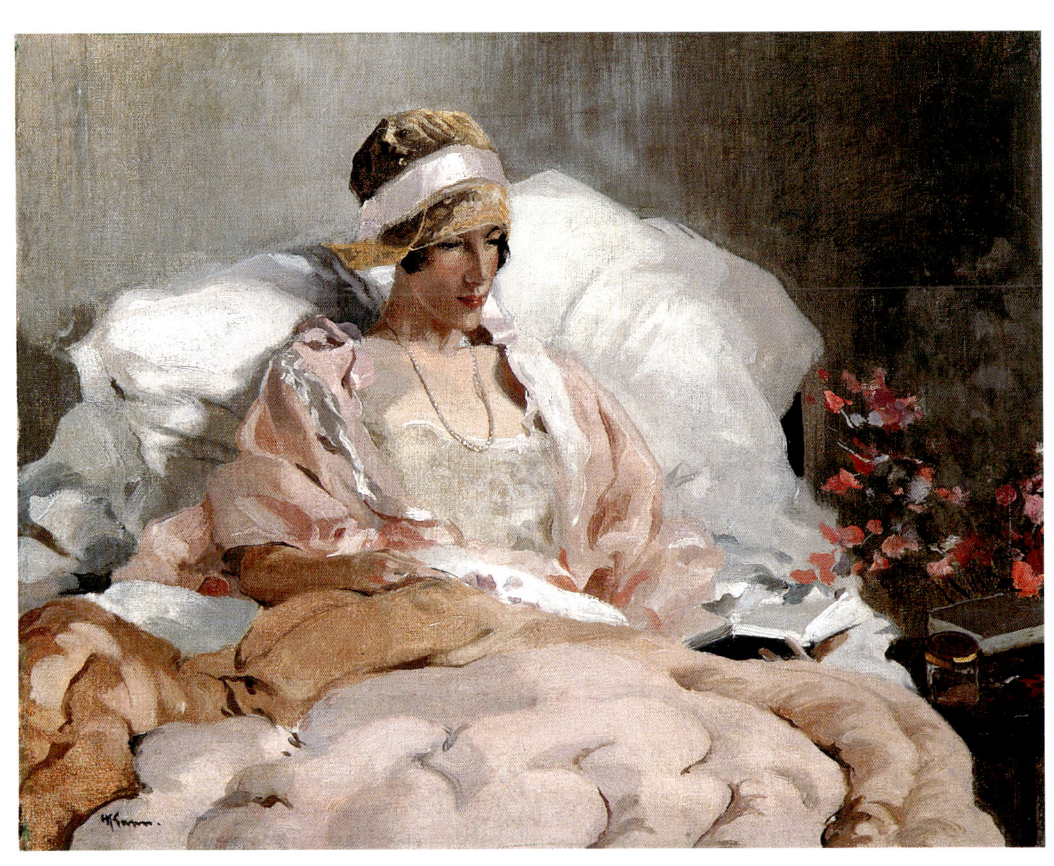

PLATE 8

GWEN IN BED

*c.*1920, CAT. 26

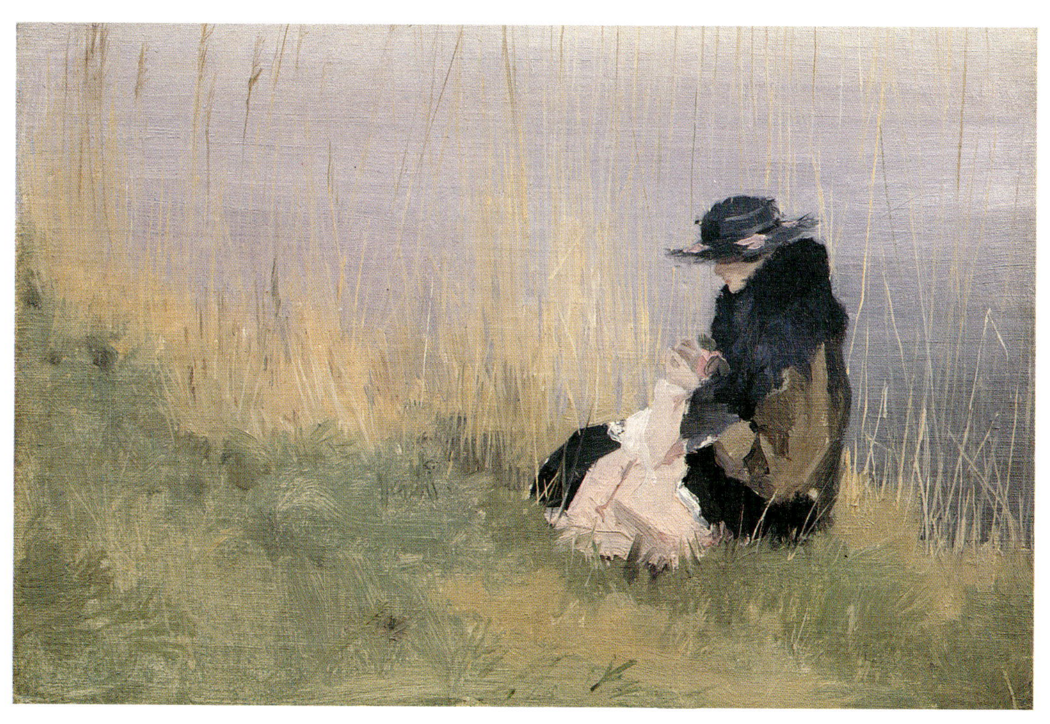

PLATE 9

GWEN ON A RIVER BANK

*c.*1920, CAT. 27

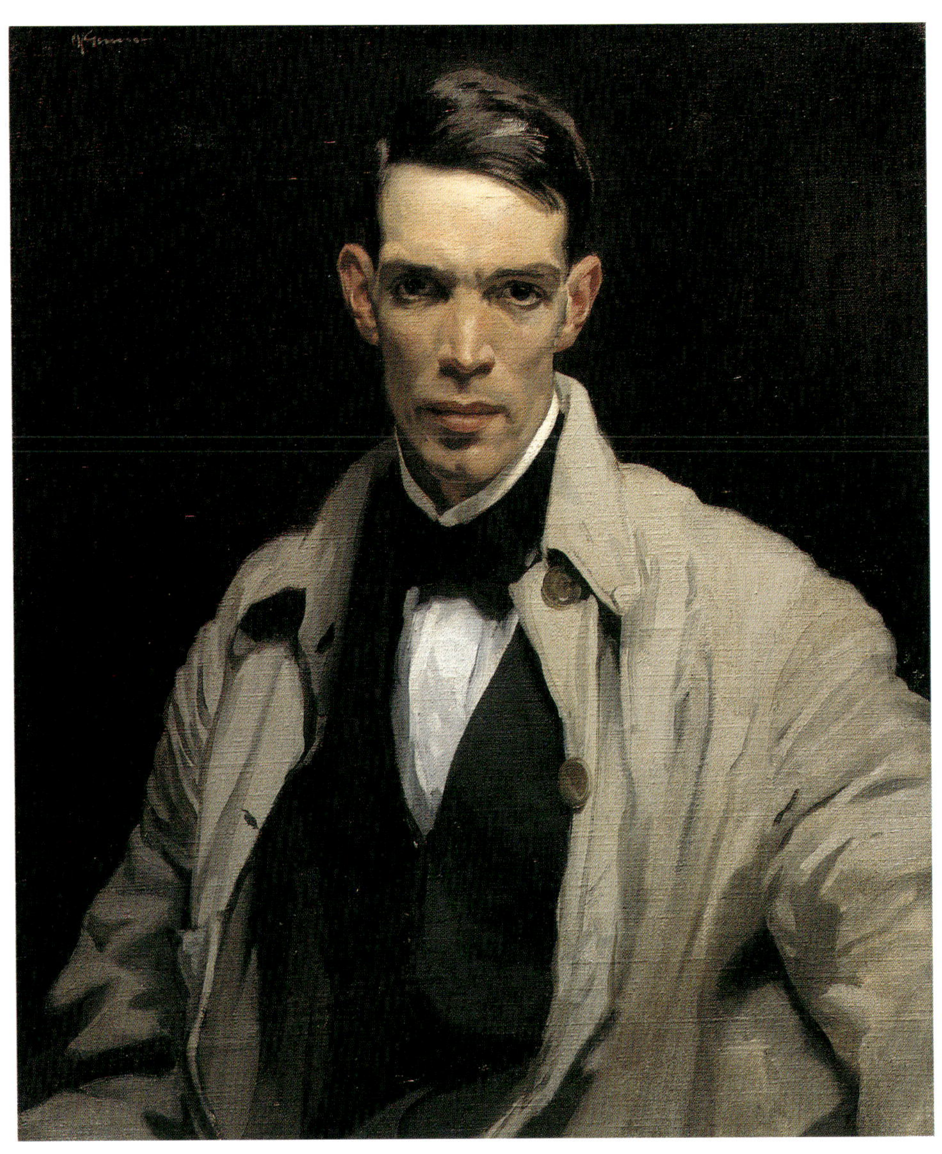

PLATE 10

SELF–PORTRAIT

1925, CAT. 30

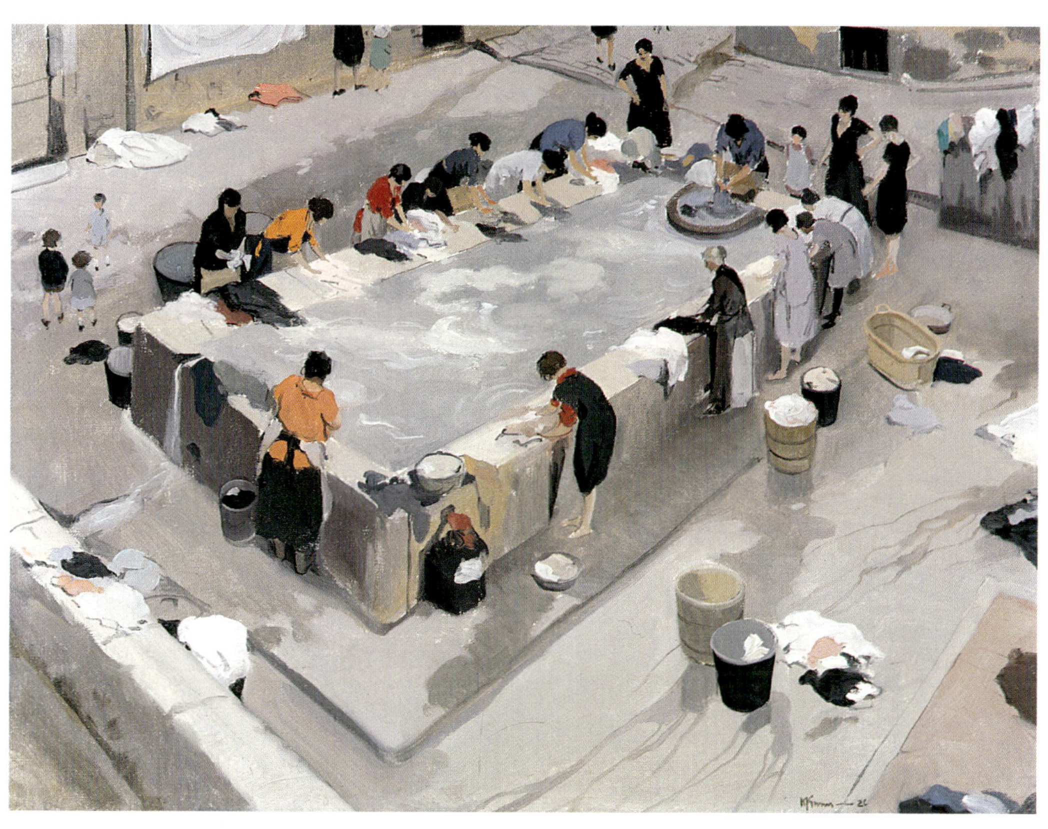

PLATE II

WASHING DAY, ANTIBES

1926, CAT. 36

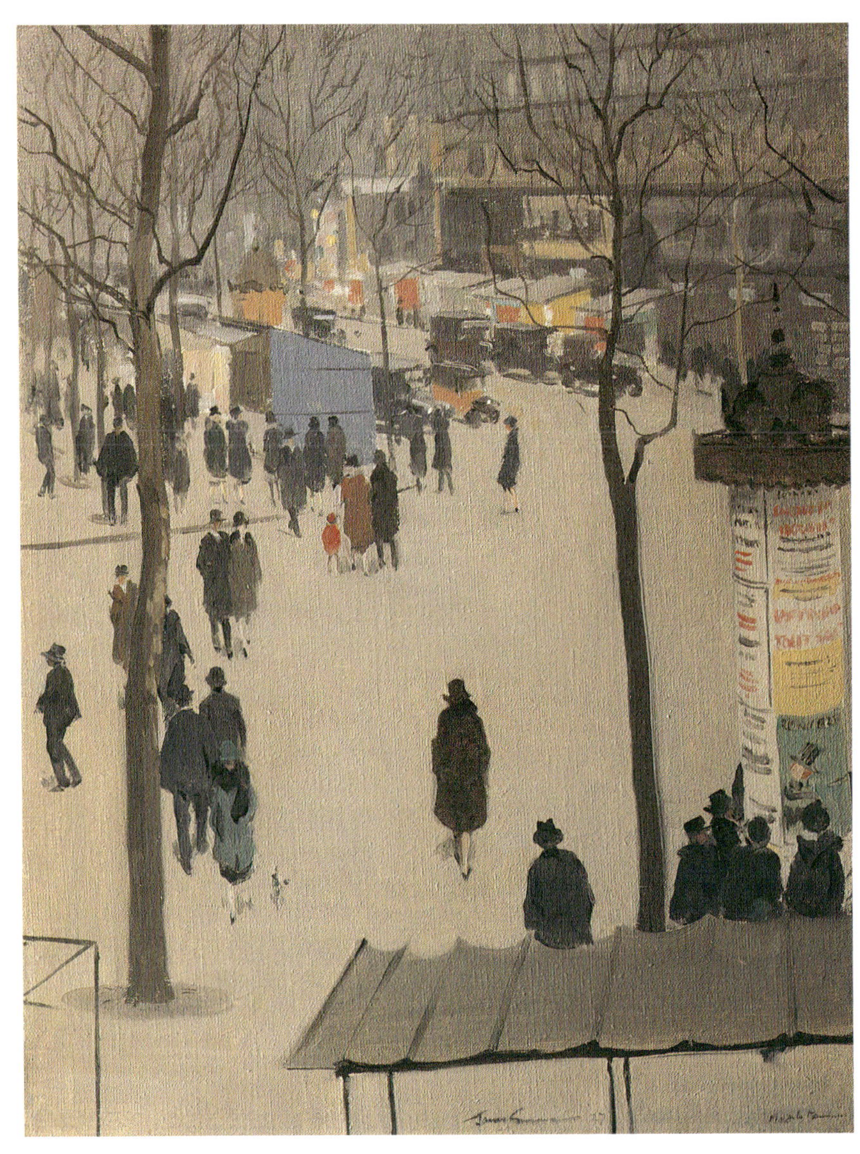

PLATE 12

PLACE DE LA MADELEINE, PARIS

1926, CAT. 38

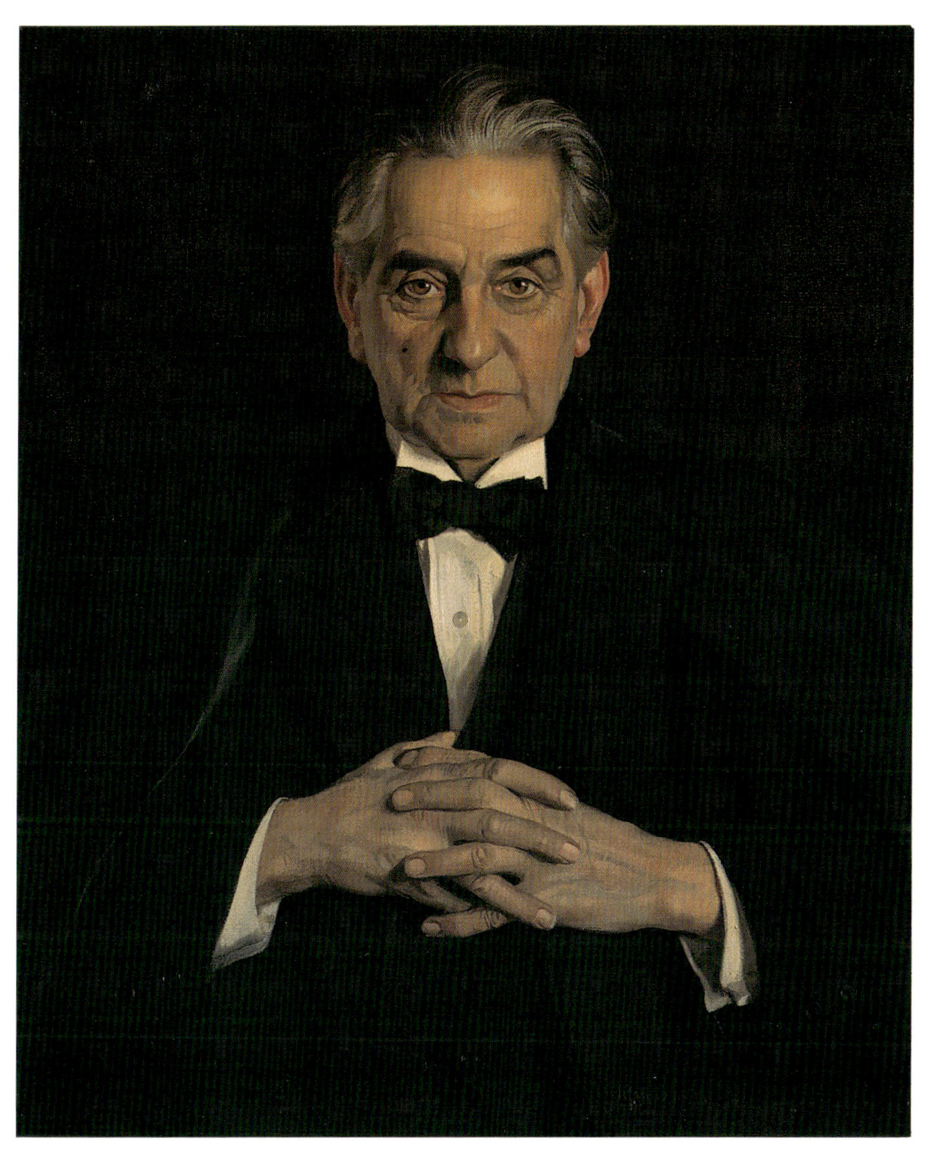

PLATE 13

CHARLES POND

1929, CAT. 43

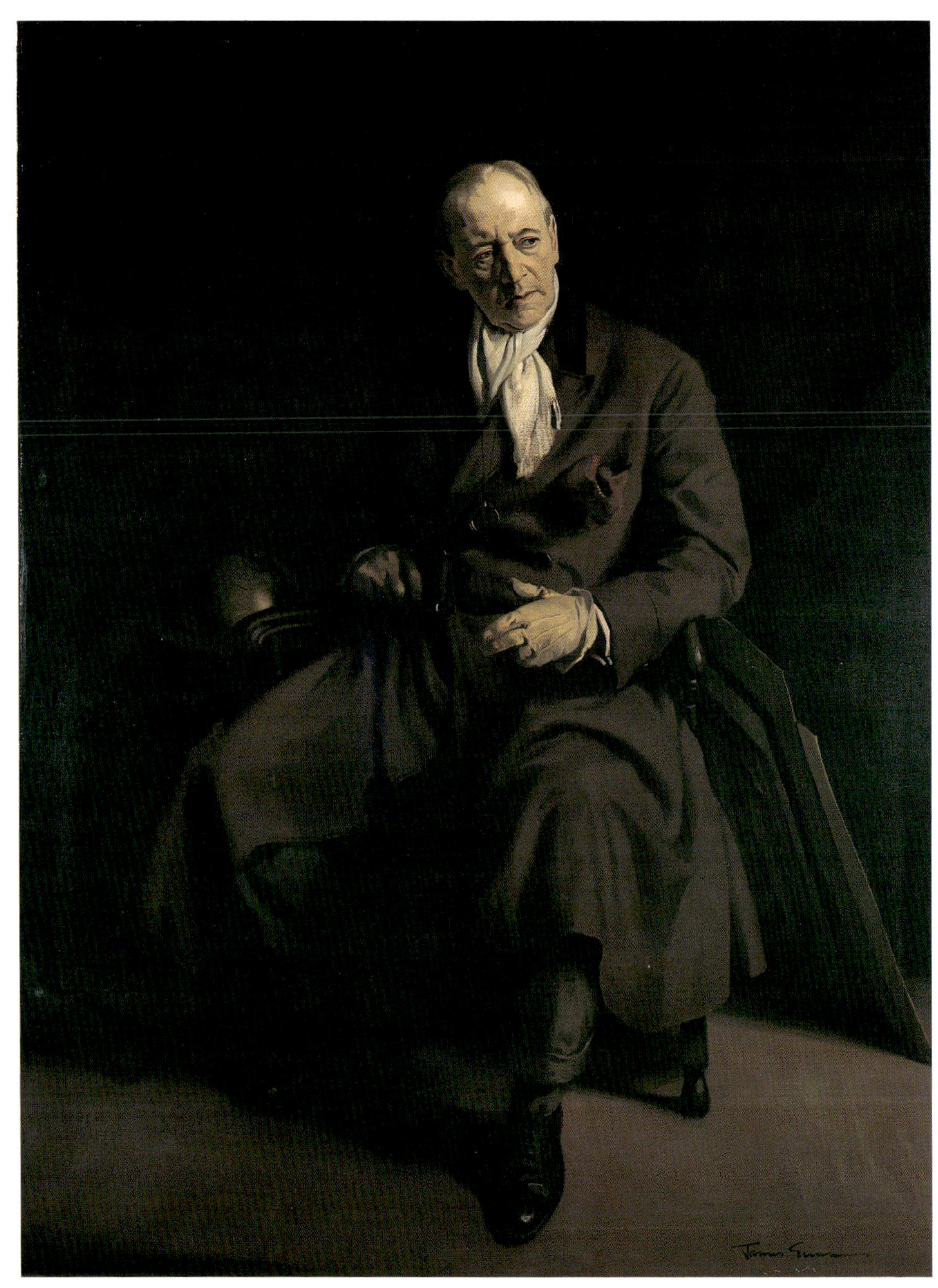

PLATE 14

JAMES PRYDE

1931, CAT. 46

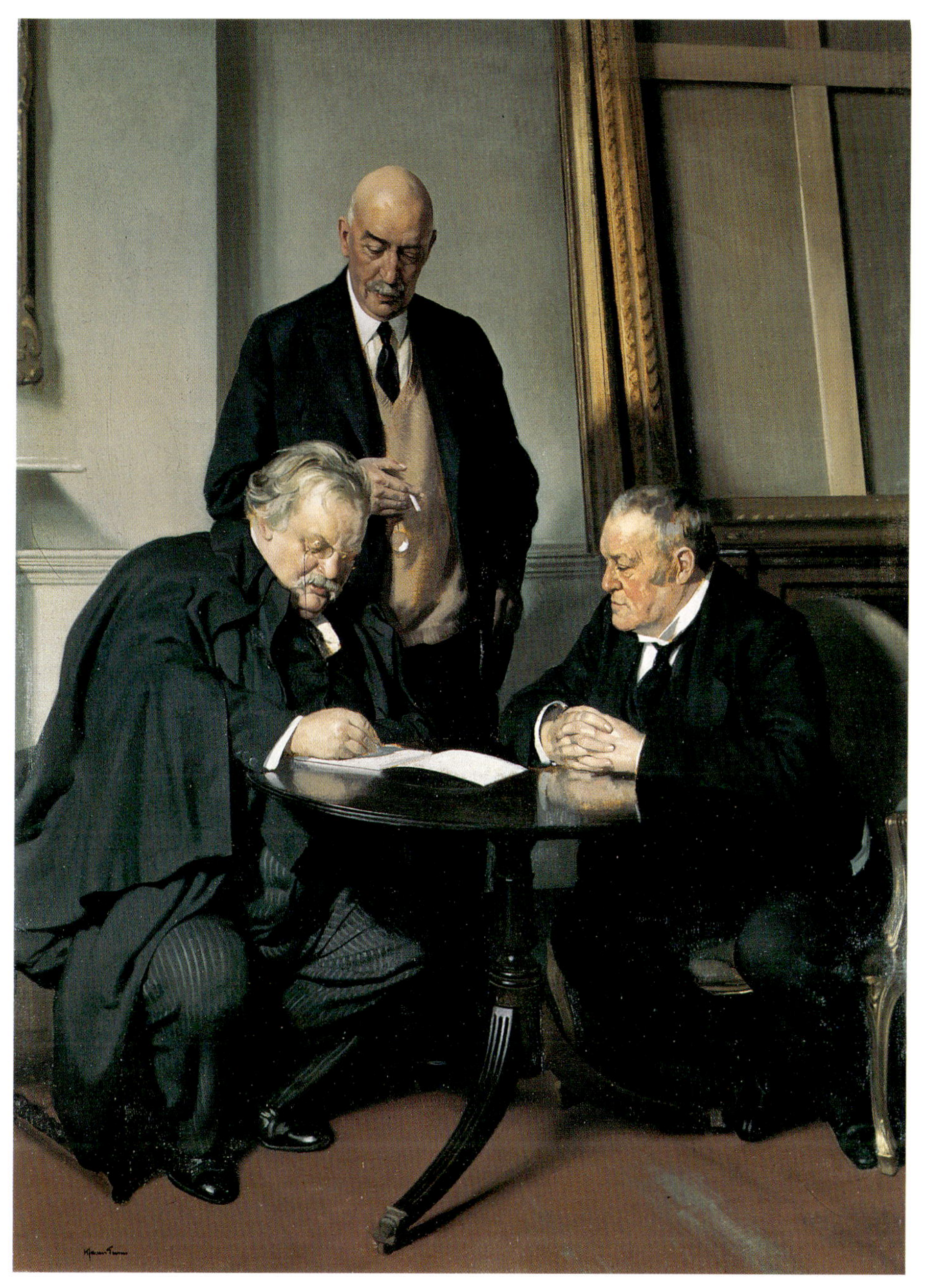

PLATE 15
CONVERSATION PIECE:
HILAIRE BELLOC, G. K. CHESTERON AND MAURICE BARING
1932, CAT. 47

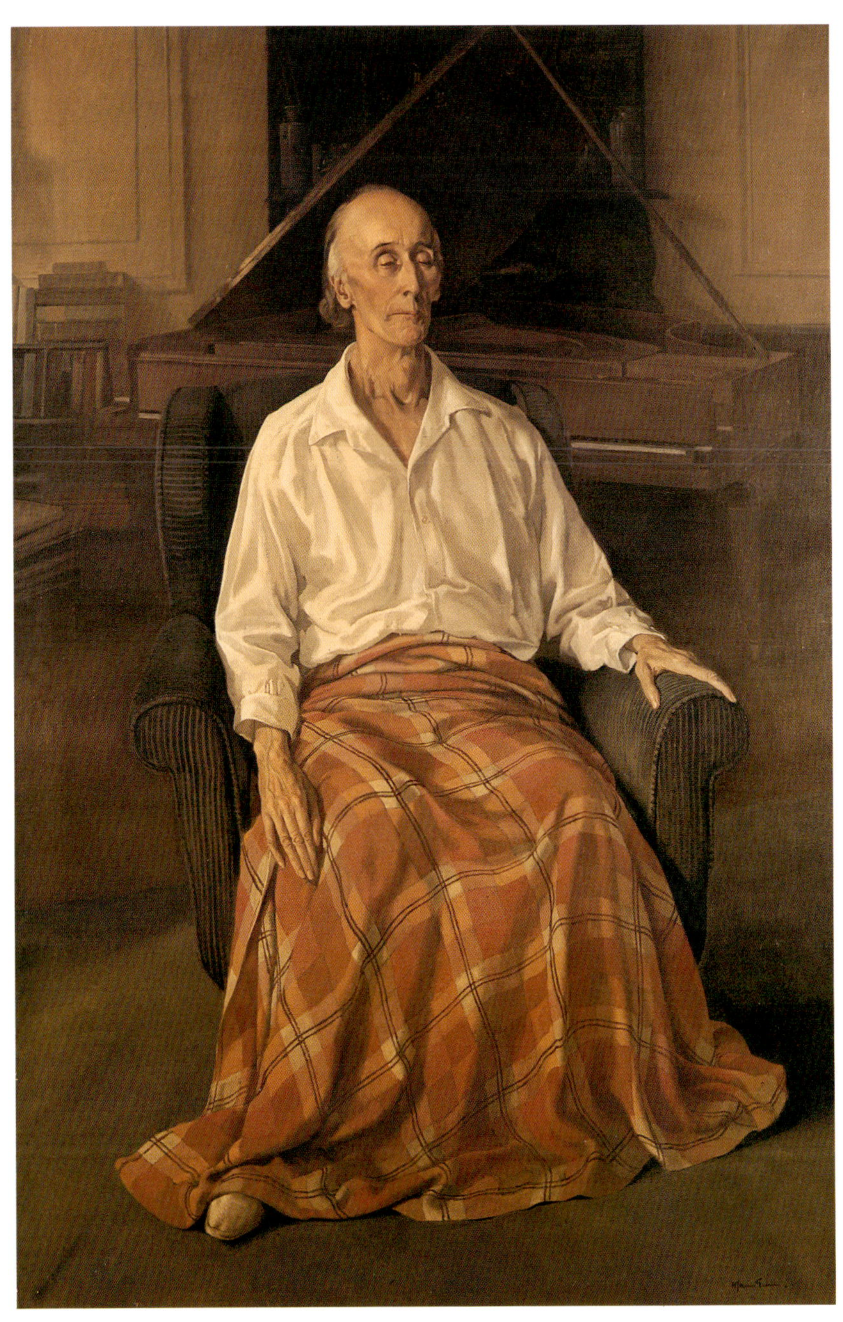

PLATE 16

DELIUS

1932, CAT. 53

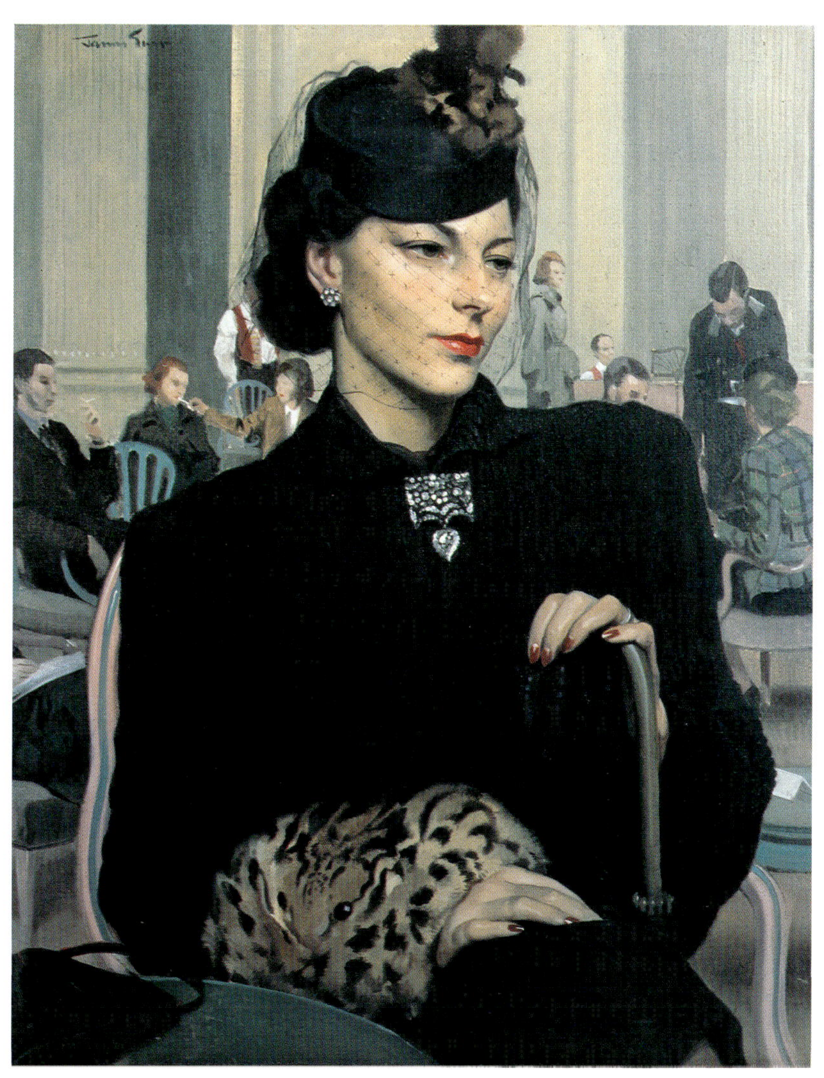

PLATE 17

PAULINE WAITING

1939, CAT. 55

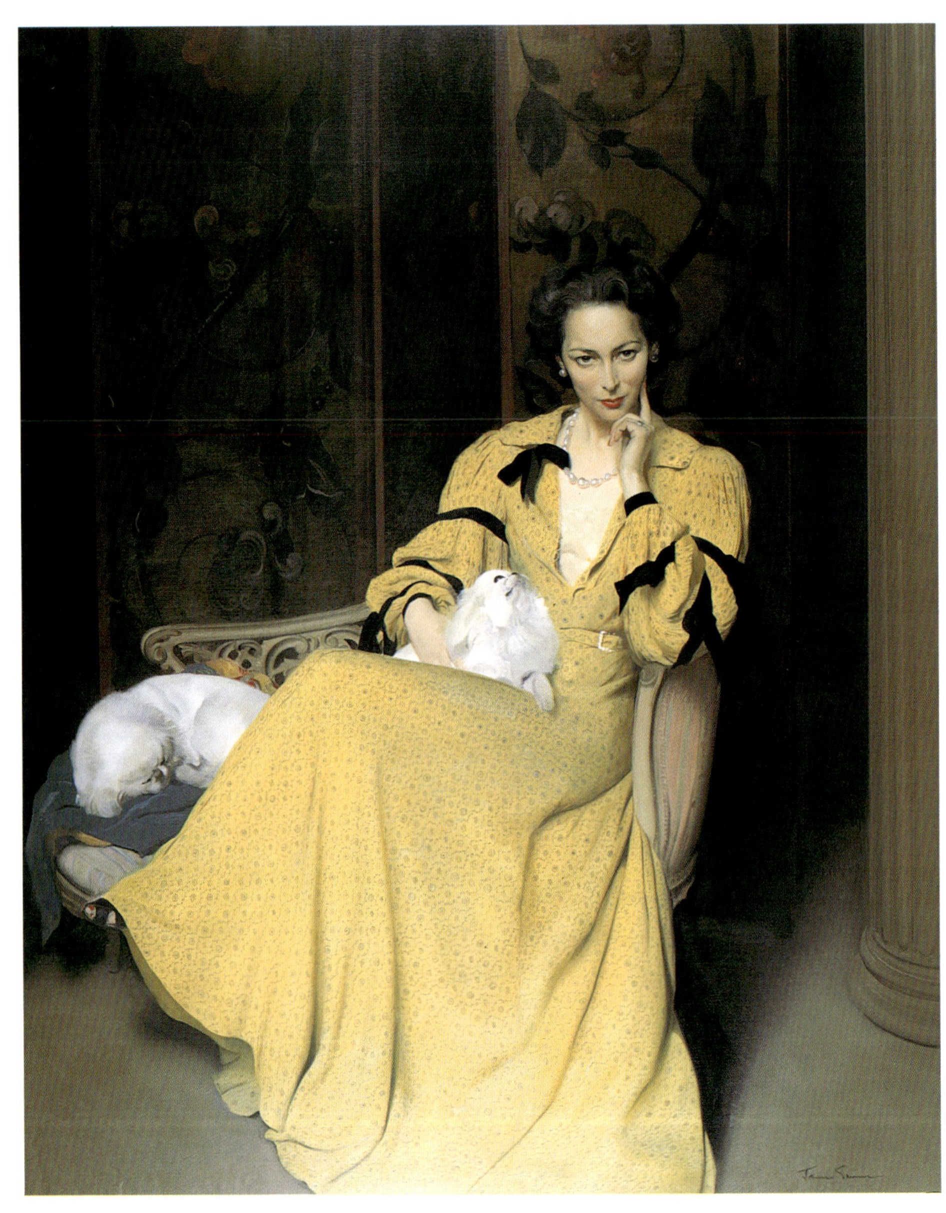

PLATE 18

PAULINE IN THE YELLOW DRESS
1944, CAT. 58

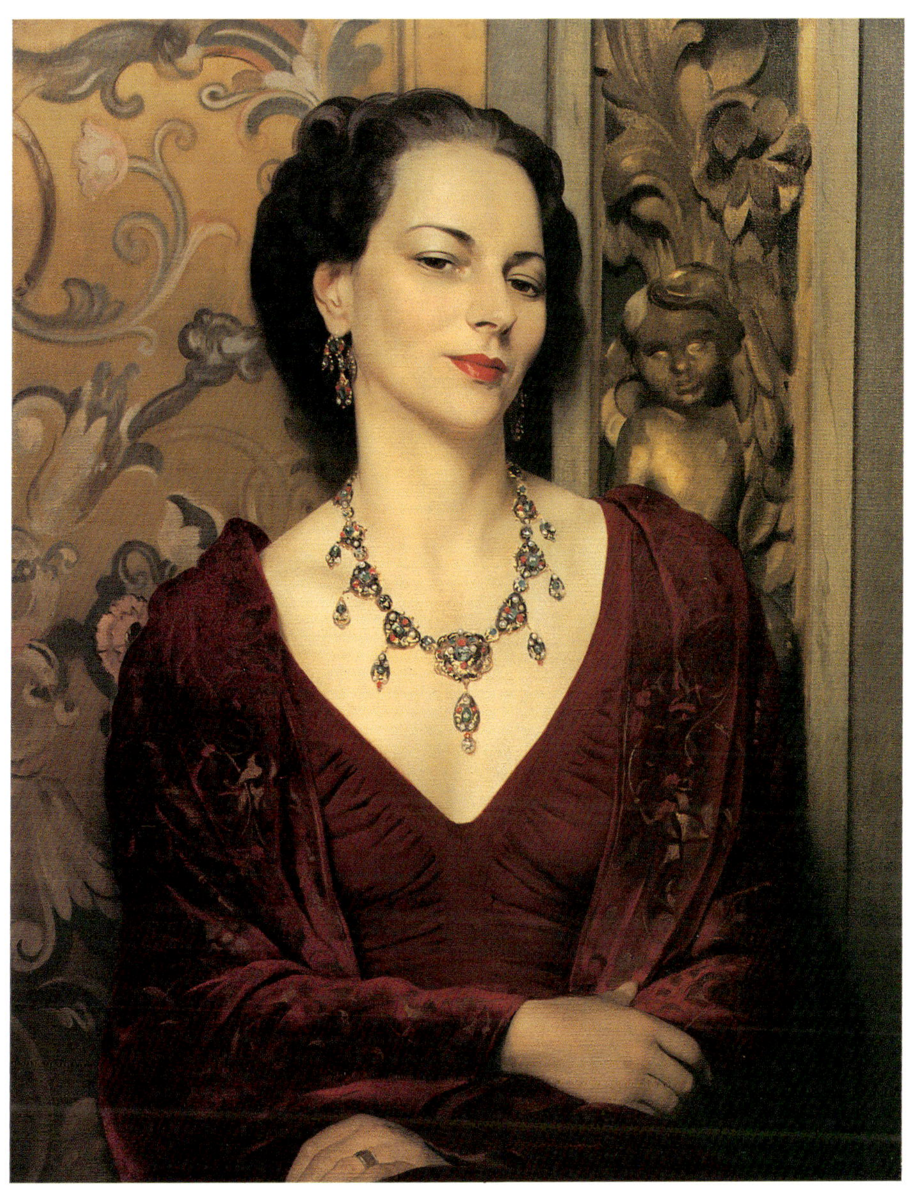

PLATE 19
PAULINE: VENETIAN SOUVENIR
1945, CAT. 59

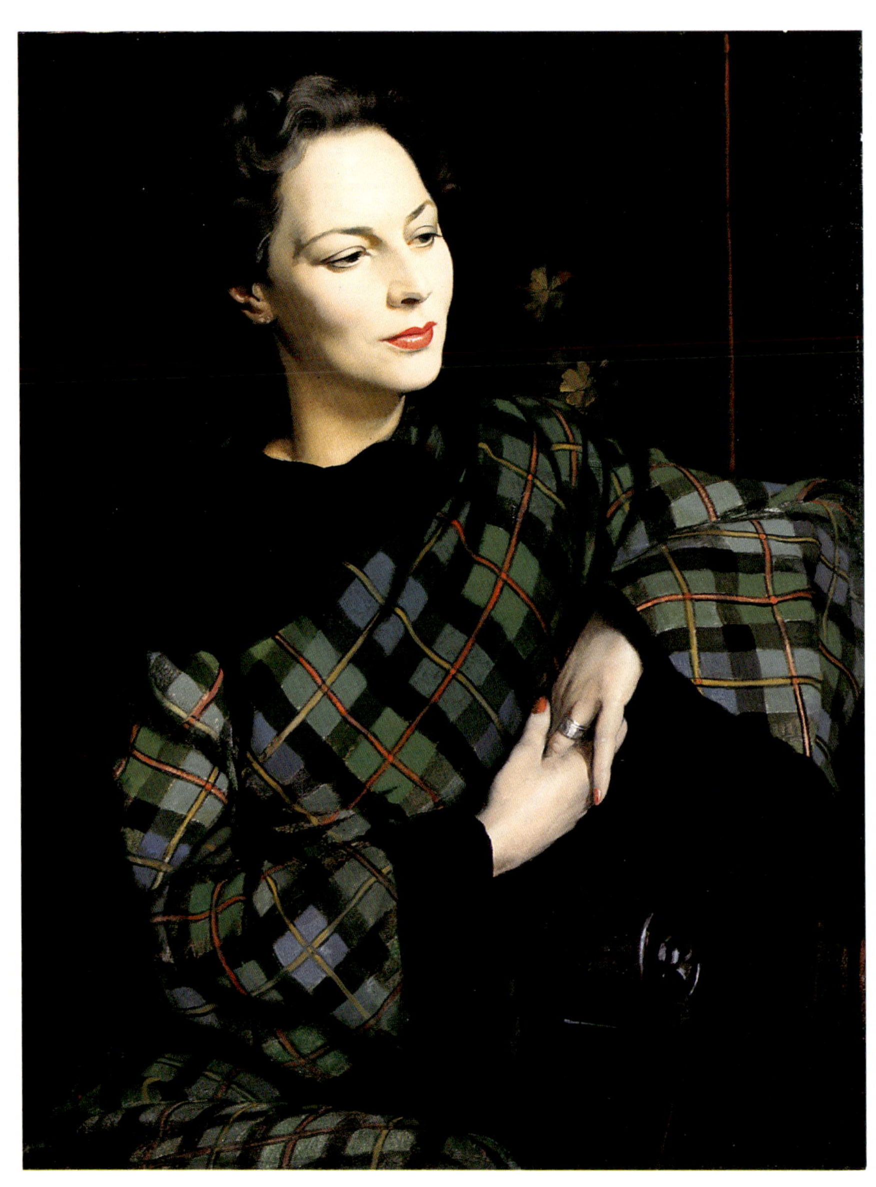

PLATE 20

PAULINE IN THE MCLEOD TARTAN

c.1946, CAT. 63

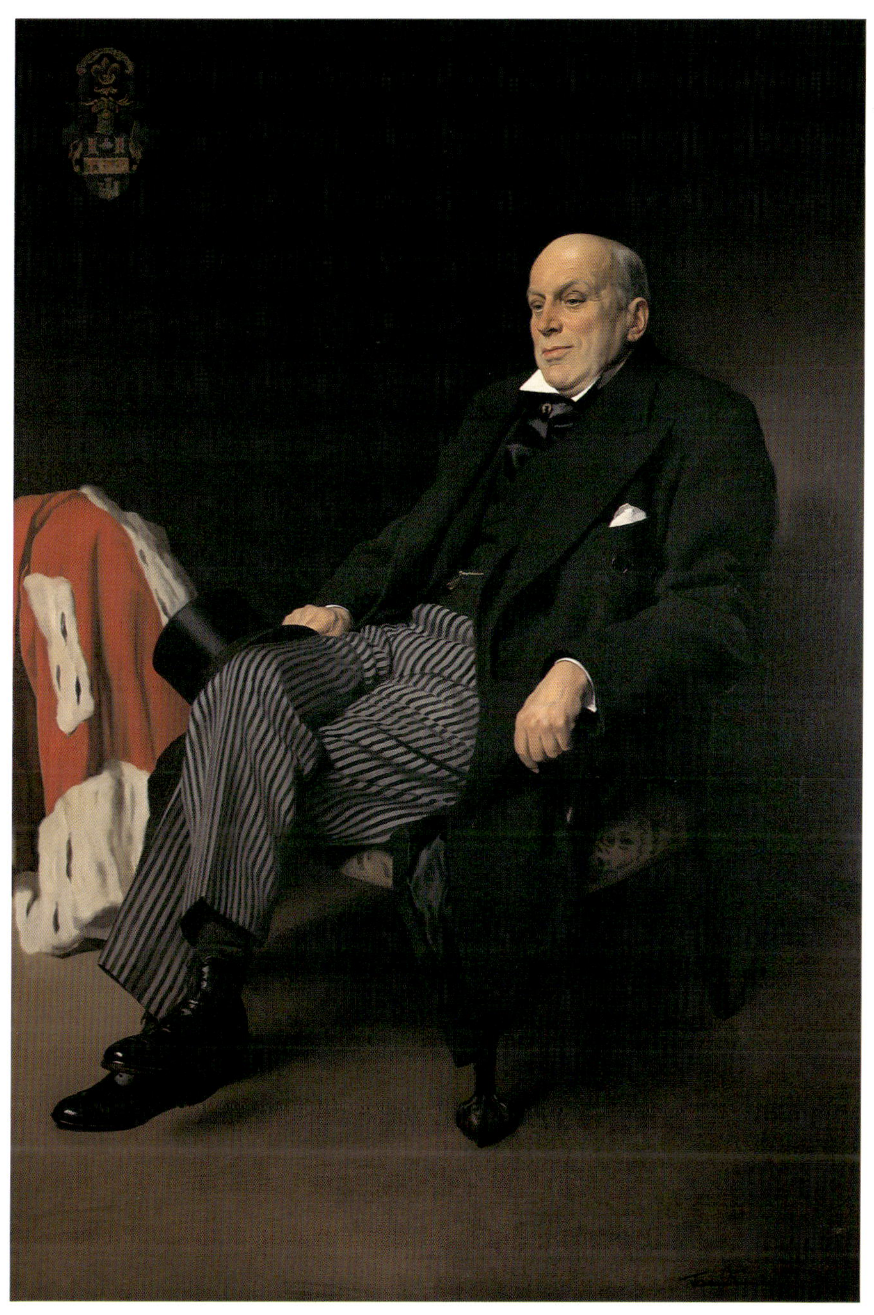

PLATE 21
SIR WILLIAM Y. DARLING
1947, CAT. 64

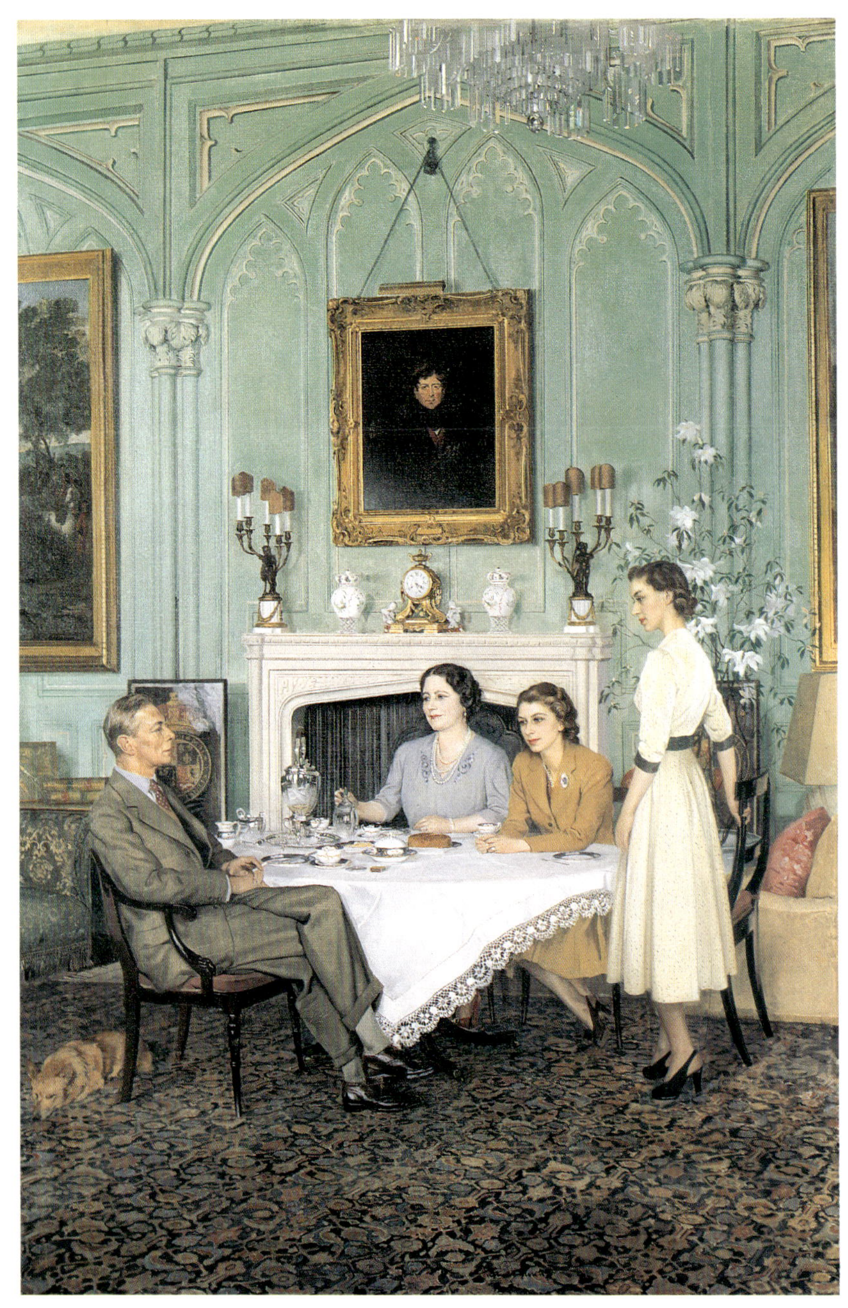

PLATE 22

CONVERSATION PIECE AT ROYAL LODGE, WINDSOR

1950, CAT. 67

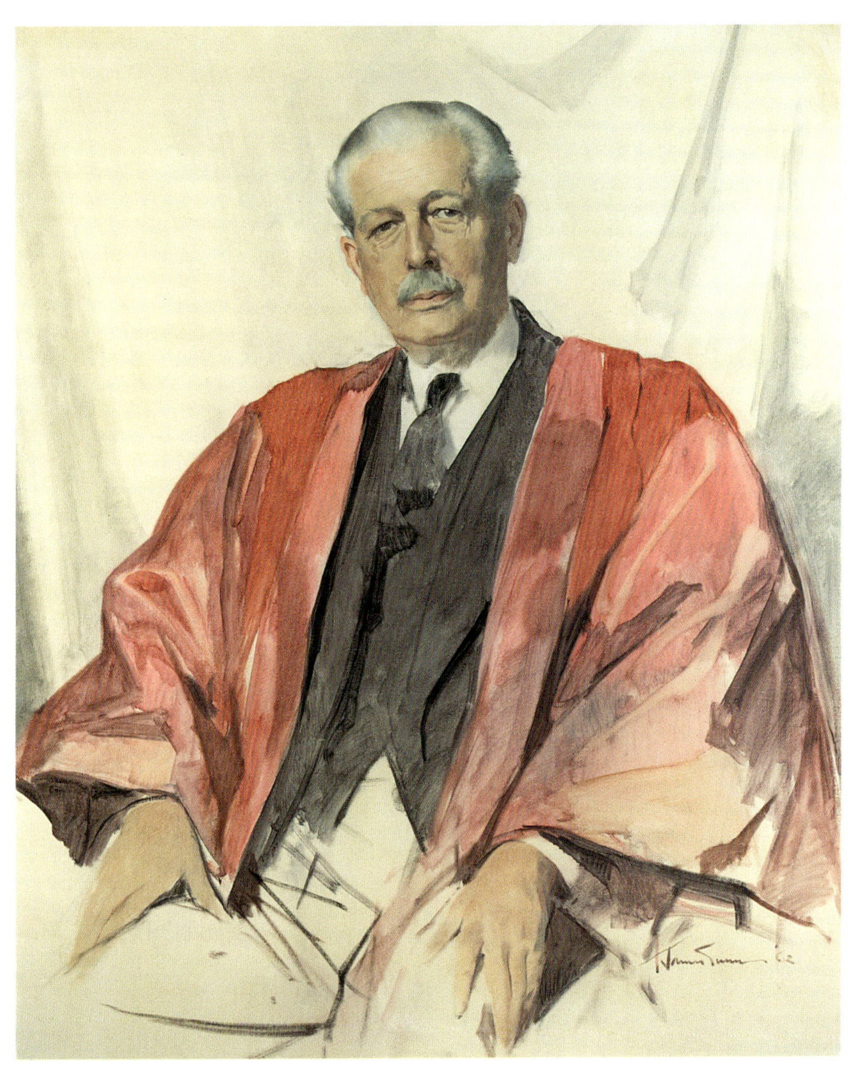

PLATE 23

THE RT HON HAROLD MACMILLAN MP

1962, CAT. 70

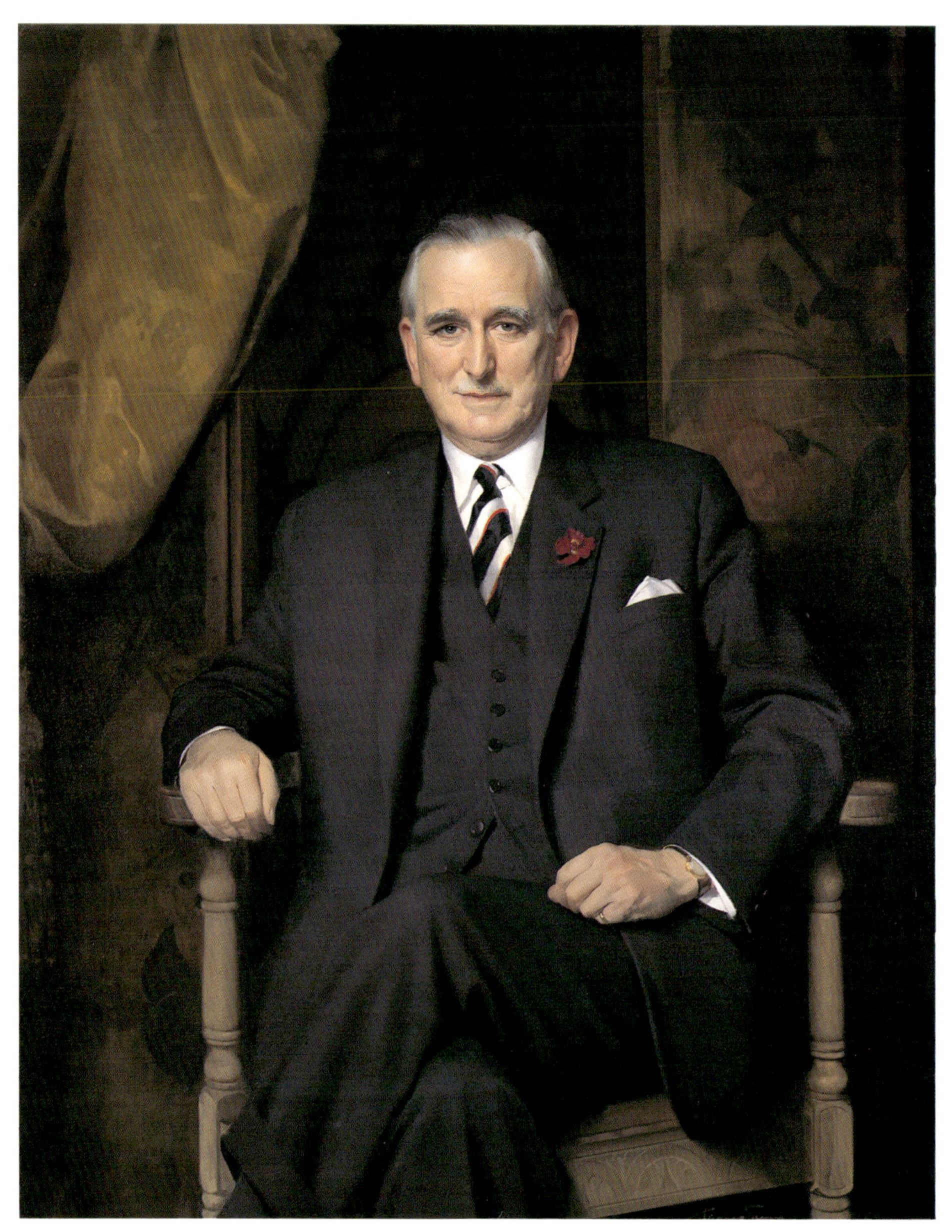

PLATE 24

LORD FRASER OF ALLANDER

1964, CAT. 71

CATALOGUE OF EXHIBITS

1

SELF-PORTRAIT

c.1910

oil on panel, 8½ × 6½ in (21.6 × 16.5 cm)

inscribed on the verso: Herbert Gunn

Private Collection

2

PRESTWICK SANDS

c.1910

oil on board, 10 × 7 in (25.4 × 17.8 cm)

Private Collection

The girl in the white dress is one of the artist's sisters.

3

2 BIS RUE PERREL, PARIS

charcoal on paper, 9½ × 6½ in (24.1 × 16.5 cm)

Private Collection

4

FROM MY WINDOW, RUE PERREL, PARIS

1912

oil on board, 9 × 5½ in (22.9 × 14 cm)

inscribed on the verso with the title

Private Collection

Gunn arrived in Paris at the end of 1911 to study at the Académie Julian under Jean-Paul Laurens. He rented a room at 2 bis rue Perrel.

5

CHILDREN PLAYING, RUE PERREL, PARIS

1912

oil on board, 9 × 6 in (22.9 × 15.2 cm)

Private Collection

6 *(plate 1)*

RUE DE NEVERS, PARIS

1912

oil on board, 8¾ × 6¼ in (22.2 × 15.9 cm)

inscribed later: Paris 1912 / To Chloe / on her 18th Birthday / JG 1948

Private Collection

7

THE GRAND PALAIS FROM LES INVALIDES, PARIS

1912

oil on board, 8½ × 10½ in (21.6 × 26.7 cm)

signed and dated; inscribed on the verso with the title

Private Collection

8

SELF-PORTRAIT

1912

oil on board, 8¼ × 5¼ in (21 × 13.3 cm)

inscribed on the verso: Portrait of myself painted in Paris, rue Perrel, in the spring of 1912 to demonstrate my facility for realism.

Private Collection

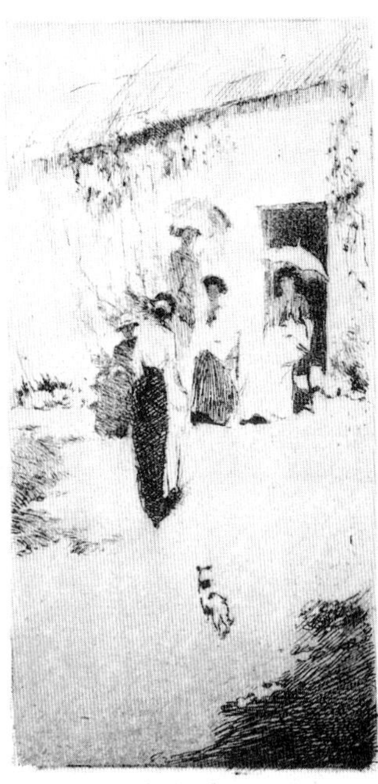

cat. 9

9

THE VISITORS
etching on paper, 4 × 2 in (10.2 × 5.1 cm)
Private Collection

10

IN THE LUXEMBOURG GARDENS
etching on paper, 3¼ × 5 in (8.3 × 12.7 cm)
Private Collection

Gunn made a number of etchings in 1912
for the London art dealer, Dowdeswell.
A complete set is in the collection of the
Hunterian Art Gallery, Glasgow.

11

BOULOGNE
1912
pencil on paper, 5½ × 3½ in (14 × 8.9 cm)
Private Collection

A postcard to the artist's brother, Charles.

12

THE ARTIST'S FATHER
1913
oil on canvas, 12 × 9 in (30.5 × 22.9 cm)
signed and dated: Herbert Gunn 1913
Private Collection

Richard Gunn was a tailor and clothier. After
his death in 1918 the family business was
carried on by James Gunn's two surviving
elder brothers. In later life Gunn described this
picture as having been painted with the
freedom of a blindfold man on the edge of a
precipice, unaware of the dangers below.

13   *(plate 2)*

THE SOCCO, TANGIER
1914
oil on board, 9 × 12 in (22.9 × 30.5 cm)
inscribed on the verso: Socco 24.4.14
exhibited: London, Thomas Agnew & Sons,
'First Impressions', 1946 (36), where Gunn
repurchased it.
Private Collection

In 1914 Gunn travelled to Tangier and back
through Gibraltar and Spain on the advice
(and at the expense) of the London dealer W.
B. Paterson. On his return he visited Paris and
Etretat.

14

THE SOCCO, TANGIER

1914
oil on board, 10 × 13½ in (25.4 × 34.3 cm)
inscribed on the verso: Tangier The Socco 28.4.14

Private Collection

15 *(plate 3)*

FROM MY WINDOW, RONDA

1914
oil on board, 9 × 13 in (22.9 × 33 cm)
inscribed on the verso with the title

Private Collection

16

LE JARDIN DES TUILERIES, PARIS

1914
oil on board, 9 × 13 in (22.9 × 33 cm)

Private Collection

17

PLACE DE LA CONCORDE, PARIS

1914
oil on board, 9 × 6 in (22.9 × 15.2 cm)
inscribed: Concorde

Private Collection

18

WINDY DAY, ETRETAT

1914
oil on board, 9¾ × 13¾ in (24.8 × 34.9 cm)

Private Collection

19 *(plate 4)*

ETRETAT

1914
oil on board, 10 × 14 in (25.4 × 35.6 cm)
signed and dated: Herbert Gunn 1914

Private Collection

20 *(plate 5)*

LA PLAGE, ETRETAT

1914
oil on canvas, 18 × 24 in (45.7 × 61 cm)

Private Collection

21 *(plate 6)*

THE EVE OF THE BATTLE OF
THE SOMME

1916
oil on canvas, 33 × 36 in (83.8 × 91.4 cm)
signed and dated: H. Gunn 1916; inscribed:
France

Dr R. T. Stanley Gunn

Gunn's younger brother Charles wrote to his
parents from France on 29 September 1916 and
described seeing this picture on a recent visit
to his brother's barracks: 'Gee Whiz it's a
knockout. In the background are sparkling
tents, in front a limpid pool, with exquisite
figures, some in the water, others reclining on
the grassy bank. Really it is a glorious thing,
and the Artist has lost none of his cunning.
The picture is framed in gold with a touch of
blue. Heb's design and the Engineer's
carpentering. Everybody loves the boy and
they'd do anything for him.'

2 2

STUDY FOR THE EVE OF THE
BATTLE OF THE SOMME

*pencil and crayon on paper, 5 × 7½ in
(12.7 × 19 cm)*

Private Collection

From a sketchbook.

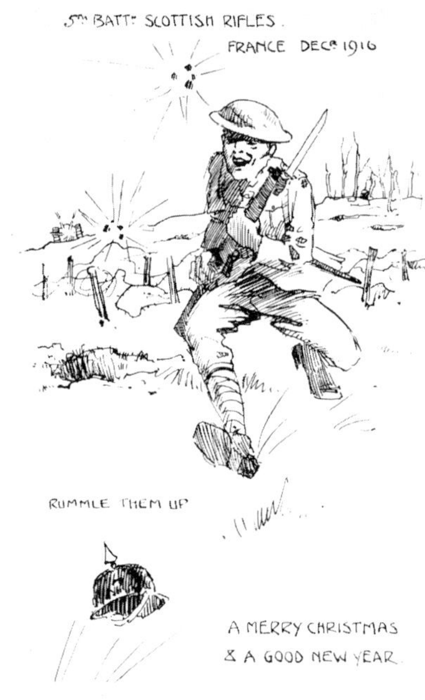

cat. 23

2 3

DESIGN FOR A CHRISTMAS CARD
FOR THE 5TH BATTALLION
SCOTTISH RIFLES

1916

pen and ink on paper, 8 × 5 in (20.3 × 12.7 cm)

Private Collection

2 4

THE ARTIST'S MOTHER

1919

oil on canvas, 30 × 25 in (76.2 × 63.5 cm)

signed: Herbert Gunn; dated on the verso

Private Collection

Thomasina Munro married Richard Gunn in
November 1875. She died on 7 June 1928.

2 5   *(plate 7)*

GWEN SEWING

c.1920

oil on canvas, 24 × 18 in (61 × 45.7 cm)

signed: H. J. Gunn

Private Collection

Gunn married his first wife Gwendoline
Hillman, widow of Guy Thorne, in 1919.
They had three daughters. The marriage was
dissolved in 1927. Thereafter she married Sir
Arthur Whinney and, following his death,
married Thomas Percival Croysdale. She died
in 1985, aged 86.

2 6   *(plate 8)*

GWEN IN BED

c.1920

oil on canvas, 14 × 18 in (35.6 × 45.7 cm)

signed: H. J. Gunn

The Fine Art Society Plc

2 7   *(plate 9)*

GWEN ON A RIVER BANK

c.1920

oil on board, 10 × 14 in (25.4 × 35.6 cm)

Private Collection

28

GWEN WITH DIANA, ELIZABETH
AND PAULINE
c.1924
oil on canvas, 18 × 14 in (45.7 × 35.6 cm)
Private Collection

29

PAULINE
1925
oil on canvas, 24 × 18 in (61 × 45.7 cm)
*signed and dated: H. J. Gunn 1925; inscribed
with the title*
*exhibited: London, Colnaghi & Co, 'Portraits
and Landscapes by H. J. Gunn', 1927 (2)*
Private Collection

A portrait of James and Gwen Gunn's
youngest daughter aged 2.

30 *(plate 10)*

SELF-PORTRAIT
1925
oil on canvas, 30 × 25 in (76.2 × 63.5 cm)
signed: H. J. Gunn
*exhibited: London, Royal Academy, 1925 (264),
as Portrait of the Artist; Glasgow, Royal
Glasgow Institute of the Fine Arts, 1925 (558)*
Private Collection

31

SELF-PORTRAIT AT THE STUDIO
WINDOW
c.1925
oil on canvas, 18 × 14 in (45.7 × 35.6 cm)
Private Collection

32

ON DECK I
1925
oil on canvas, 14 × 18 in (35.6 × 45.7 cm)
signed: H. J. Gunn
Private Collection

In 1925 Gunn sailed to Argentina on board the
Arlanza and returned immediately on the
Andes.

33

ON DECK II
1925
oil on canvas, 14 × 18 in (35.6 × 45.7 cm)
signed: H. J. Gunn
Private Collection

34

HOWE'S BATHING STATION
c.1925
oil on canvas, 14 × 18 in (35.6 × 45.7 cm)
signed: H. J. Gunn
*exhibited: London, Colnaghi & Co, 'Portraits
and Landscapes by H. J. Gunn', 1927 (22)*
Private Collection

35

OLD WATERLOO BRIDGE, LONDON
c.1926
oil on canvas, 18 × 24 in (45.7 × 61 cm)
signed: H. J. Gunn
*exhibited: (possibly) London, Colnaghi & Co,
'Portraits and Landscapes by H. J. Gunn', 1927*
Private Collection

36 *(plate 11)*

WASHING DAY, ANTIBES

1926
oil on canvas, 18 × 24 in (45.7 × 61 cm)
signed and dated: H. J. Gunn 1926
exhibited: London, Colnaghi & Co, 'Portraits and
Landscapes by H. J. Gunn', 1927 (13); Glasgow,
T. &R. Annan & Sons, 1927 (22)
Private Collection

37

ON THE RAMPARTS, ANTIBES

1926
oil on canvas, 24 × 18 in (61 × 45.7 cm)
signed and dated: H. J. Gunn 1926; inscribed with
the title; inscribed on the verso: Antibes £42.00
exhibited: London, Colnaghi & Co, 'Portraits and
Landscapes by H. J. Gunn', 1927 (6 or 39)
Private Collection

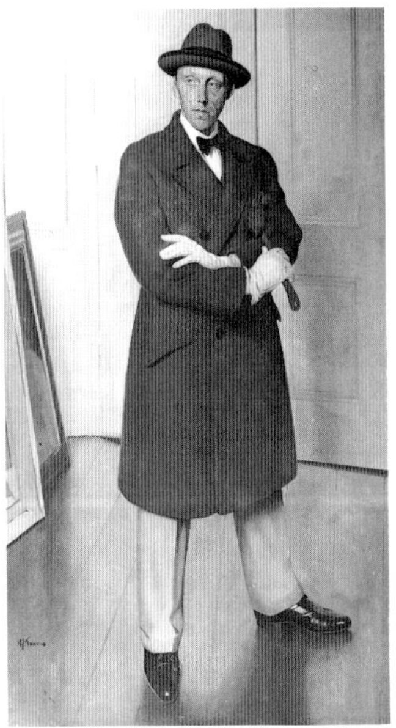

cat. 41

38 *(plate 12)*

PLACE DE LA MADELEINE, PARIS

1926
oil on canvas, 18 × 14 in (45.7 × 35.6 cm)
signed (probably later): James Gunn; inscribed
with the title
exhibited: London, Colnaghi & Co, 'Portraits and
Landscapes by H. J. Gunn', 1927 (34); Glasgow,
T. & R. Annan & Sons, 1927 (11)
Private Collection

39

PLACE DE LA CONCORDE, PARIS

1926
oil on canvas, 14 × 18 in (35.6 × 45.7 cm)
signed: H. James Gunn; inscribed on the verso with
the title
exhibited: (possibly) London, Colnaghi & Co,
'Portraits and Landscapes by H. J. Gunn', 1927
Private Collection

40

LES PECHEURS

1926
oil on canvas, 18 × 14 in (45.7 × 35.6 cm)
exhibited: London, Colnaghi & Co, 'Portraits and
Landscapes by H. J. Gunn', 1927 (5)
Private Collection

41

W. O. HUTCHISON

c.1926
oil on canvas, 80 × 45 in (203.2 × 114.3 cm)
signed: H. J. Gunn
exhibited: Edinburgh, Royal Scottish Academy,
1927 (303)
The Fine Art Society Plc

Hutchison and Gunn met at Edinburgh College of Art in 1910. They remained close friends for the rest of their lives. Hutchison was made President of the Royal Scottish Academy in 1950. Gunn exhibited a second portrait of him, wearing the robes and chains of that office, at the Royal Academy, London in 1952.

42

THE OLD OLIVE MILL

1928/9
oil on canvas, 18 × 14 in (45.7 × 35.6 cm)
signed: H. J. Gunn; inscribed on the verso: The Old Olive Mill / H. James Gunn/ 12 Bedford Gardens, London, W8/50 guineas / £52.10
exhibited: London, The Fine Art Society, 'Paintings of Rome Etc', 1929 (17)

Private Collection

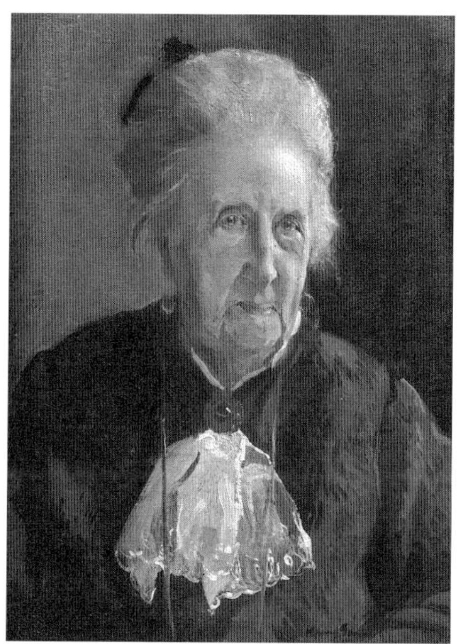

cat. 45

43 *(plate 13)*

CHARLES POND

1929
oil on canvas, 30 × 25 in (76.2 × 63.5 cm)
signed and dated: H. James Gunn 1929
exhibited: London, Royal Academy, 1929 (189)

The Savage Club

Pond, who was born Joseph Pattle, was an actor, comedian, sometime writer, star of the music hall stage, and a regular at the Savage Club in Adelphi Terrace where Gunn met him early in 1929. On 15 March, Gunn described this picture in a letter to his future wife, Pauline Miller: '… Bill Hutchison says it is the finest thing I've ever done and makes him feel like giving up his job.'

44

MABEL MONTGOMERIE

1930
oil on canvas, 23½ × 17½ in (60 × 44.5 cm)
signed: James Gunn

Mrs Ian Lang

Mabel Montgomerie was a friend of the Gunns in Glasgow and is portrayed in fancy dress for a party at Glasgow School of Art.

45

MRS OLIVIA GRINDLAY

1930
oil on board, 10 × 8 in (25.4 × 20.3 cm)
signed: H. James Gunn
exhibited: London, Grafton Galleries, 1930; London, Thomas Agnew & Sons, 'First Impressions', 1946 (14)

Mrs Edward Grindlay

Olivia Grindlay was the mother of Gunn's friend and patron Edward Grindlay. She died in May 1930, aged 83.

46 *(plate 14)*

JAMES PRYDE

1931

oil on canvas, 80 × 60 in (203.2 × 152.4 cm)

signed: James Gunn

*exhibited: London, Royal Society of Portrait
Painters, 1932 (110); London, Barbizon House,
'London Pictures and Recent Portraits', 1933
(17); London, Royal Academy, 1941 (291);
Edinburgh, Royal Scottish Academy, 'James
Pryde', 1949 (29); Edinburgh, Scottish National
Gallery of Modern Art, 'James Pryde', 1992
(109)*

*Private Collection on loan to the Scottish National
Portrait Gallery*

Gunn opened the 1949 Arts Council exhibition
of Pryde's work and described this portrait of
his friend as 'the most characteristic of the
three' that he had painted of him: '… he was
one of the most impressive figures I have ever
seen. Tall, he was over 6 feet, he had a noble
head and carried himself with immense dignity.'
He was also near destitution for much of his
later life and Gunn was among those friends
who helped him through his declining years.

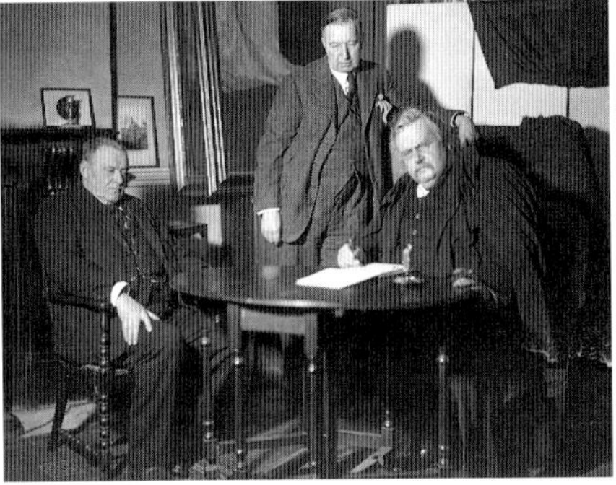

fig. 13

The first sitting for *Conversation Piece*. Edward Grindlay,
in the centre, posed for Maurice Baring who was abroad.

47 *(plate 15)*

CONVERSATION PIECE: HILAIRE
BELLOC, G. K. CHESTERTON AND
MAURICE BARING

1932

oil on canvas, 59½ × 43½ in (151.1 × 110.5 cm)

signed: H. James Gunn

*exhibited: London, Royal Academy, 1932 (430)
and 1965 (151); London, Knoedler & Co, 'Portraits
by James Gunn', 1935 (4); Edinburgh, Royal
Scottish Academy, 1933 (178)*

National Portrait Gallery, London

The idea for a portrait of the three writers (left
to right: Chesterton, Baring, Belloc) came to
Gunn in 1930 at a dinner to celebrate Belloc's
60th birthday. He recalled the episode in a
speech to University College School (25 July
1962): ' … "Splendid," said Belloc, "you shall
show it in the Royal Academy, and it will help to
sell our books." Maurice Baring said, "I will sit
for you tomorrow," which he did … but two
years passed and I could never get them
together. In January 1932 I wrote to Belloc
asking when he could come and bring his
friends. He replied that he was going to be in
town for a month with Gilbert (Chesterton),
Maurice was away in Malta and would be back in
a week, but that he would bring Gilbert to the
studio and perhaps I could make a start. I
arranged with a friend who was the right shape
to deputise for Maurice and on that Sunday I
made my first sketches' (fig. 13). The picture
was shown at the Academy in 1932 and bought
before the official opening by George Balfour
for £1,500. The picture was lent to the National
Portrait Gallery and Hilaire Belloc enjoyed the
rare privilege for a living person, previously
reserved for members of the Royal Family and
Winston Churchill, of seeing his image hanging
on the gallery walls. The usual rule at that time

was that subjects should have been ten years dead. *Conversation Piece* was given to the National Portrait Gallery in November 1960.

48

FIRST IMPRESSION FOR CONVERSATION PIECE

1932
oil on canvas, 18 × 14 in (45.7 × 35.6 cm)
Mrs Edward Grindlay

Edward Grindlay, '… a friend of the right shape', takes the place of Maurice Baring (standing).

49

CARTOON FOR CONVERSATION PIECE

1932
pencil and charcoal on paper, 60 × 44 in (152.4 × 111.8 cm)
signed: James Gunn
exhibited: London, Barbizon House, 'London Pictures and Recent Portraits', 1933 (35)
Mervyn Herbert

50

HILAIRE BELLOC

1932
charcoal on paper, 20 × 15 in (50.8 × 38.1 cm)
signed: H. James Gunn; inscribed: HB
exhibited: London, Barbizon House, 'London Pictures and Recent Portraits', 1933 (36)
The Fine Art Society Plc

51

G. K. CHESTERTON

1932
pencil on paper, 15 × 10 in (38.1 × 25.4 cm)
The Fine Art Society Plc

52

MAURICE BARING

1932
red crayon on paper, 18 × 13 in (45.7 × 33 cm)
signed: H. J. Gunn; inscribed: Maurice Baring
The Fine Art Society Plc

53 (plate 16)

DELIUS

1932
oil on canvas, 72 × 48 in (182.9 × 121.9 cm)
signed: H. James Gunn
exhibited: London, Royal Academy, 1933 (192) and 1965 (153)
Bradford Art Galleries and Museums

In March 1947 Gunn opened the Spring Exhibition at Cartwright Hall, Bradford, and, in his speech, described the conception of his plans for a portrait of Frederick Delius at Sir Thomas Beecham's Delius festival at the Queen's Hall in 1929: '… it was at these concerts that I first saw the tragic figure of the great composer as he sat listening in the Circle, and felt that here was a great portrait that cried out to be painted … about a year later I was in the north-west room of the old Savage Club talking of my desire to paint Delius when the late Norman O'Neill remarked that "Fred" was his oldest friend, and so I had my contact. It was at the end of August 1932 that I finally went to the peaceful village of Grez-sur-Loing. Delius, who was not far from the end, was very infirm, paralysed and blind and reluctant to sit … the only time I could get sittings was in the afternoon between four and six. I had my canvas near to the window to get what light there was and worked feverishly during the two hours, for as soon as the church clock struck six he became restive and it was time for me to go. I have never painted a picture that caused me so much physical fatigue.' The picture was bought from the Royal Academy in 1933 by George Balfour for £1,250 and subsequently sold by his heirs to Bradford in 1946.

54

HILAIRE BELLOC

c.1934
oil on canvas, 85 × 46 in (215.9 × 116.8 cm)
signed: James Gunn
exhibited: London, Royal Academy, 1939 (386); Glasgow, Royal Glasgow Institute of the Fine Arts, 1939 (457)
Private Collection

55　*(plate 17)*

PAULINE WAITING

1939
oil on canvas, 30 × 25 in (76.2 × 63.5 cm)
signed: James Gunn
exhibited: Edinburgh, Royal Scottish Academy, 1940 (145) ; Glasgow, Royal Glasgow Institute of the Fine Arts, 1962 (85); London, Royal Academy, 'The Edwardians and After 1900– 1950', 1990 (27)
Royal Academy of Arts, London

Presented by Gunn to the Royal Academy as his Diploma Work on 10 October 1961. Pauline is shown sitting in the lobby of Claridge's Hotel, London.

56

STUDY FOR PAULINE WAITING

pen and ink on paper, 5 × 4 in (12.7 × 10.2 cm)
Private Collection

From a sketch book.

57

SELF-PORTRAIT

1941
oil on panel, 4¼ × 3½ in (10.8 × 8.9 cm)
signed: James Gunn
exhibited: London, Royal Academy, 1941 (375)
Private Collection

58　*(plate 18)*

PAULINE IN THE YELLOW DRESS

1944
oil on canvas, 50 × 40 in (127 × 101.6 cm)
signed: James Gunn
exhibited: London, Royal Academy, 1944 (244); Glasgow, Royal Glasgow Institute of the Fine Arts, 1949 (447); London, Royal Society of Portrait Painters, 1965
Harris Museum and Art Gallery, Preston

59　*(plate 19)*

PAULINE: VENETIAN SOUVENIR

1945
oil on canvas, 26 × 23 in (66 × 58.4 cm)
signed: James Gunn
exhibited: London, Royal Academy, 1945 (498); Glasgow, Royal Glasgow Institute of the Fine Arts, 1945 (87); London, Royal Academy, 1965 (336)
Private Collection

Pauline is wearing a coat of crimson velvet made from cloth bought directly from Mario Fortuny in Venice in 1938. The title is a conscious recollection of Venice and of the days before the outbreak of the Second World War.

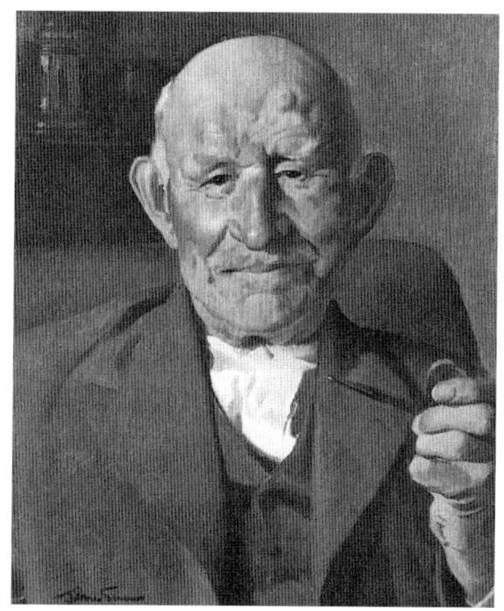

cat. 60

60

OLD JOHN CONNELL

c.1945
oil on canvas, 18½ × 15½ in (47 × 39.4 cm)
signed: James Gunn
exhibited: London, Royal Society of Portrait
Painters, 1964 (33); Glasgow, Royal Glasgow
Institute of the Fine Arts, 1964 (379)
Private Collection

John Connell was a retired farmer and the
Gunns' next door neighbour at Carsethorn on
the Solway Firth.

61

BLACK ROBSON

c.1945
oil on canvas, 18 × 14 in (45.7 × 35.6 cm)
signed: James Gunn
exhibited: London, Thomas Agnew & Sons,
'First Impressions', 1946 (12)
Private Collection

62

BOB STITT

c.1945
oil on canvas, 18 × 14 in (45.7 × 35.6 cm)
inscribed on the verso with the title
Private Collection

Bob Stitt and Black Robson were both
fishermen and Carsethorn neighbours.

63   (plate 20)

PAULINE IN THE MCLEOD TARTAN

c.1946
oil on canvas, 30 × 25 in (76.2 × 63.5 cm)
Private Collection

64   (plate 21)

SIR WILLIAM Y. DARLING CBE MC DL
JP LLD MP, LORD PROVOST OF THE
CITY OF EDINBURGH 1941–1944

1947
oil on canvas, 60 × 40 in (152.4 × 101.6 cm)
signed and dated: James Gunn '47
exhibited: London, Royal Academy, 1947 (237)
Edinburgh City Museums and Art Galleries

W. Y. Darling was MP for South Edinburgh
and Lord Provost of the city during the
Second World War. This portrait was
commissioned at the end of his term to hang in
the City Chambers. Reviewing the Royal
Academy pictures in April 1947, Eric Newton
commented in the *Sunday Times* that it was '…
remarkable and arresting, chiefly for the
painting of the sitter's trousers.'

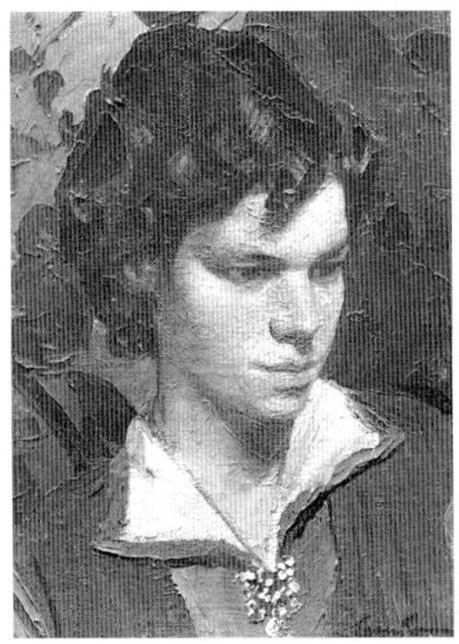

cat. 65

65

CHLOE GUNN

1948
oil on board, 8 × 6 in (20.3 × 15.2 cm)
signed: James Gunn

Private Collection

This portrait of Chloë Gunn, and the following portrait of her brother Paul, children of James and Pauline, are rare examples of Gunn working with a palette knife.

66

PAUL

1950
oil on board, 5¾ × 4¼ in (14.6 × 10.8 cm)
signed and dated: J G 15.1.50

Private Collection

67   *(plate 22)*

CONVERSATION PIECE AT ROYAL
LODGE, WINDSOR

1950
oil on canvas, 60 × 40 in (152.4 × 101.6 cm)
exhibited: London, Royal Academy, 1950 (245)

National Portrait Gallery, London

The sitters are (left to right) King George VI, Queen Elizabeth (The Queen Mother), Princess Elizabeth (Queen Elizabeth II) and Princess Margaret. Gunn's introduction to royal portraiture had come in 1944 with a commission to paint the King. It was followed in 1946 when the Middle Temple commissioned him to paint Queen Elizabeth. The informal setting of *Conversation Piece at Royal Lodge, Windsor* was suggested by the King. The picture was commissioned by the National Portrait Gallery.

68

DAME MYRA CURTIS

1954
oil on canvas, 40 × 30 in (101.6 × 76.2 cm)
signed: James Gunn

The Principal and Fellows of Newnham College, Cambridge

Dame Myra Curtis was Principal of Newnham College, Cambridge, from 1942 to 1954.

69

A MEETING OF THE SOCIETY OF
DILETTANTI

1959
oil on canvas, 47 × 54 in (119.4 × 137.2 cm)
exhibited: London, Royal Academy, 1959 (376)

Society of Dilettanti

The Society of Dilettanti has its origins in the eighteenth-century Hellfire Club. Its members, all distinguished lovers of the fine arts, meet regularly in Brooks's Club, London. In former years they met in the St James's Club which is the setting of Gunn's portrait. The members are (left to right) –

Standing: Victor Goodman, Sir Malcolm
Sargent, The Duke of Wellington, James
Gunn. Seated: Lord Harlech, Lord Methuen,
Lord Hinchingbrooke, Louis Clarke, Sir
Charles Clay, Sir Dougal Malcolm, Lord
Ilchester, Lord Spencer, Sir Alan Barlow, Sir
James Mann, James Laver.

70   *(plate 23)*

THE RIGHT HON HAROLD
MACMILLAN MP

1962
oil on canvas, 44 × 36 in (110 × 91.4 cm)
signed and dated: James Gunn 62

The Macmillan Trust

Gunn was first commissioned to paint the
Prime Minister, Harold Macmillan (in the
robes of Chancellor of Oxford University), by
the Carlton Club in 1960. Macmillan's fellow
Balliol men in Parliament subsequently
commissioned a second portrait of the Prime
Minister wearing his Balliol gown. This

portrait bears a typed label on the reverse,
signed by Gunn and dated 18 March 1963:
'This sketch was made at the first sitting for
the Balliol portrait on July 20 1962. It seemed
so complete that I decided to leave it, and copy
the arrangement on a new canvas for the
second sitting James Gunn 18.3.63.' Gunn
gave this version to the sitter who was later
ennobled as the Earl of Stockton.

71   *(plate 24)*

LORD FRASER OF ALLANDER
BT LLD JP

1964
oil on canvas, 50 × 40 in (127 × 101.6 cm)
signed: James Gunn
exhibited: London, Royal Academy, 1964 (189)

Scottish National Portrait Gallery

Sir Hugh Fraser, Chairman of the House of
Fraser, was knighted in 1961 and created Lord
Fraser of Allander in 1964, the year of this
portrait and the last year of Gunn's life.

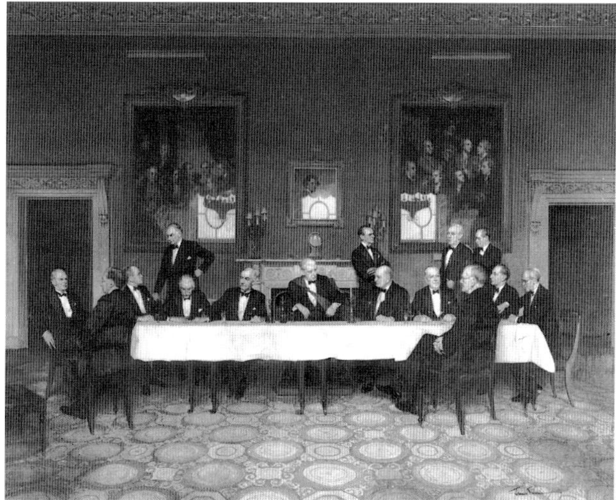

cat. 69

BIBLIOGRAPHY

SOLO EXHIBITION CATALOGUES

1919

London, Wm. B. Paterson, *Pictures by H. J. Gunn*

Glasgow, T. & R. Annan & Sons, *Paintings by H. J. Gunn*

1920

Glasgow, T. & R. Annan & Sons, *Paintings by H. J. Gunn*

1927

London, P. & D. Colnaghi & Co, *Portraits and Landscapes by H. J. Gunn*

Glasgow, T. & R. Annan & Sons, *Paintings by H. J. Gunn*

1929

London, The Fine Art Society, *Paintings of Rome etc. by H. J. Gunn*

1933

London, Barbizon House, *London Pictures and Recent Portraits by H. James Gunn*

1935

London, M. Knoedler & Co, *Portraits by James Gunn*

1946

London, Thomas Agnew & Sons Ltd, *First Impressions by James Gunn*

1973

Edinburgh, Daniel Shackleton, *Herbert James Gunn 1893–1964, Portrait and Landscape Painter*

GENERAL

Billcliffe, Roger, *The Glasgow Boys*, London, John Murray, 1985

Billcliffe, Roger , *The Royal Glasgow Institute of Fine Arts 1867–1869 Vol. II*, Glasgow, Woodend Press, 1991

Exhibition catalogue, *Munnings v. The Moderns*, Manchester City Art Gallery, 1987

Exhibition catalogue, *The Edwardians and After*, MaryAnne Stevens, ed., London, The Royal Academy of Arts, 1988

Exhibition catalogue, *James Pryde*, Edinburgh, National Galleries of Scotland, 1992

Fenby, Eric, *Delius – As I Knew Him*, London, G. Bell & Sons, 1936

Hudson, Derek, *James Pryde*, London, Constable, 1949

Hutchison, S. C., *The History of the Royal Academy 1768–1968*, London, Chapman & Hall, 1968

de Laperriere, Charles Baile, ed., *The Royal Scottish Academy Exhibitors 1826–1990 Vol. III*, Calne, Hilmarton Manor Press, 1991

National Portrait Gallery Complete Illustrated Catalogue, London, National Portrait Gallery, 1981

The Royal Academy Exhibitors 1905–1970 Vol. III, Wakefield, E. P. Publishing, 1978

Scharf, Aaron, *Art and Photography*, London, Penguin, 1968

ARTICLES ON JAMES GUNN

Glasgow Citizen, 2 June 1913; *Glasgow Herald*, 23 March 1914; *Morning Post*, 13 June 1919; *Bazaar*, 28 June 1919; *The Times*, 24 June 1919; *Daily Telegraph*, 25 June 1919; *Dundee Courier*, 4 February 1923; *The Sporting Times*, 11 May 1929; *Daily Record*, 4 May 1931; H. Granville Fell, 'Portraits by James Gunn', *Apollo*, September 1931; *Daily Express*, 16 November 1931; *The Times*, 17 February 1932; *Daily Telegraph*, 30 April 1932; *News of the World*, 30 April 1933; *The Times Weekly Educational Supplement*, 4 May 1933; *Glasgow Citizen*, 15 May 1933; *Apollo*, June 1933; Sybil Vincent, 'In the Studio of James Gunn', *The Studio*, December 1936; *The Bystander*, No 1882 vol CXLV 1940; *The Tatler*, 7 February 1940; *The Sketch*, 13 March 1940; *Observer*, 4 May 1941; *The Sphere*, April 1944; *Daily Mail*, 29 April 1944 ; *The Tatler and Bystander*, 10 May 1944; *The Illustrated London News*, 24 October 1944; *Daily Dispatch*, 5 May 1945; *Daily Express*, 15 May 1946; *Punch*, 14 May 1947; *The Spectator*, 9 May 1947; *Daily Mail*, 30 April 1949; *7 Tagge* (Germany), May 1950; *Dundee Advertiser*, 22 September 1950; *Scottish Field*, August 1951; *Daily Worker*, 3 May 1952; *Daily Mail*, 2 May 1953; *Scottish Field*, February 1953; *Daily Mirror*, 1 May 1954; *Manchester Guardian*, 1 May 1954; *Daily Telegraph*, 1 May 1954; *The Times*, 1 May 1954; *Evening Standard*, 4 May 1954; *Time Magazine*, 10 May 1954; *The Star*, 6 May 1955; *Daily Mail*, 20 November 1956; *Glasgow Evening Citizen*, 25 September 1957; *The Scotsman*, 23 August 1958; *Glasgow Herald*, 4 December 1958; *Woman's Own*, 3 October 1959; *Yorkshire Post*, 29 January 1961; *Daily Mail*, 23 February 1961; *The Illustrated London News*, 4 March 1961; *Daily Telegraph*, 11 April 1963; *The Scotsman*, 11 May 1963; *Manchester Guardian*, 1 January 1965; *Daily Telegraph*, 1 January 1965; *Daily Telegraph*, 12 April 1965; *Country Life*, 6 May 1965

BOOKS ILLUSTRATED BY GUNN

Richard Gunn, *The Social Trinity*, Glasgow 1908

The 10th Battalion, The Cameronians: A Record and a Memorial 1914–1918, Edinburgh 1918

Various covers and illustrations for *Open Air, Out of Doors* and *The Illustrated Sporting and Dramatic News c.1921*

CATALOGUE RAISONNÉ

A *catalogue raisonné* of James Gunn's work is currently under preparation. Any information would be gratefully received and should be sent to James Holloway, Scottish National Portrait Gallery, 1 Queen Street, Edinburgh EH2 1JD.